Girl, Get Up

YOU WERE NEVER MEANT TO STAY DOWN

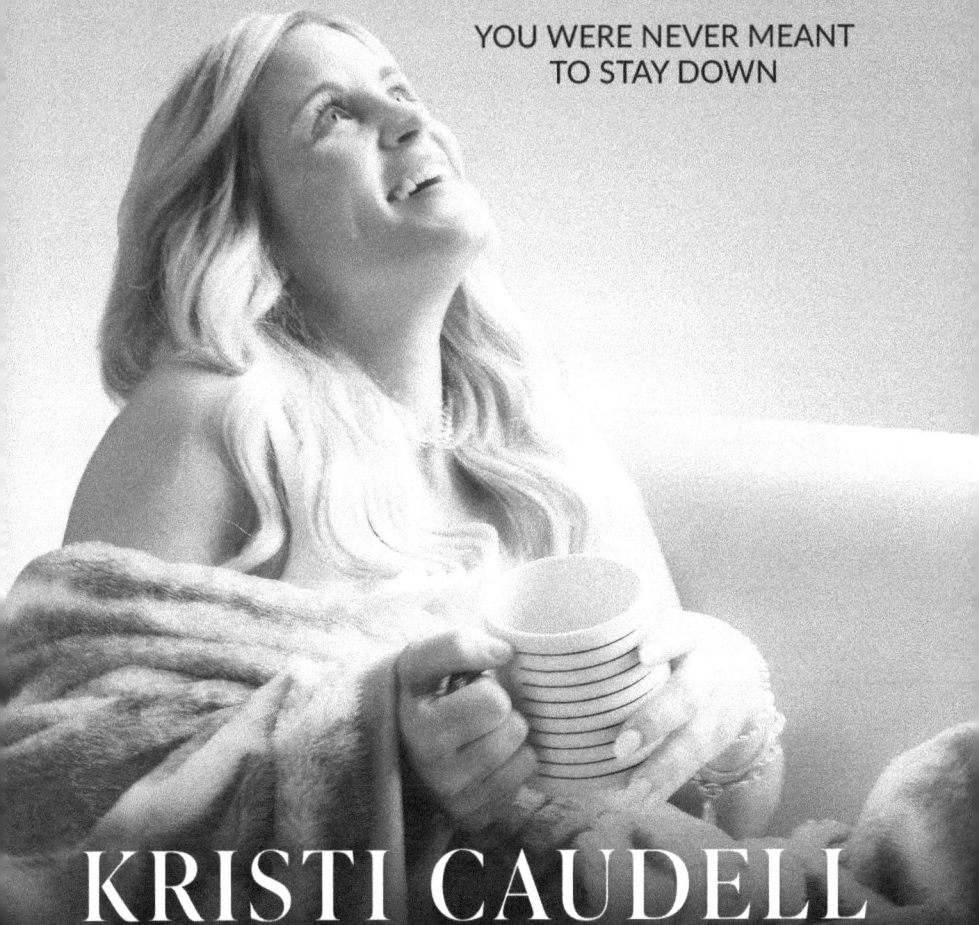

KRISTI CAUDELL

Donald Trump's *The Apprentice*, Season 4

with Joanna K. Hunt

SILVERSMITH
PRESS

Published by Silversmith Press–Houston, Texas
www.silversmithpress.com

ISBN 978-1-967386-30-7 (Hardcover Book)
ISBN 978-1-967386-26-0 (Softcover Book)
ISBN 978-1-967386-27-7 (eBook)

DEDICATION

To my mother, Debbie Caudell, whose strength and faith shaped me.

To my father, Don Caudell, whose lessons still guide me.

To Lindsay, my best friend and sister in spirit—I carry you with me always.

To Mary Elizabeth, my heart and my constant. You have seen me grow more than anyone, living this story with me day by day. Through every season, every triumph, and every heartbreak, you have been there. Your love, patience, and quiet strength mean more to me than words can ever express.

To Catelyn—especially you. You were raised by a child, yet I could not be prouder of the woman you are today. Your strength, wisdom, and grace inspire me every day.

To the coaches and teachers who saw something in me before I ever did.

And to those who are still standing with me today—you know who you are. Your love, support, and unwavering belief in me have carried me through life's hardest moments.

This book is for you as much as it is for me.

CONTENTS

Foreword by Joanna Hunt.. vii

Introduction: We're in This Together ix

1. Performance Hiding Pain... 1

2. Flatlining Dreams...13

3. Cleats to the Fire..25

4. Trumping Reality..37

5. Finding the Voice I Never Lost.......................................51

6. Behind Closed Doors...61

7. Looking for Love, Finding Myself....................................75

8. Follow the Trailblazers...83

9. The Right to Remain Silent . . . but Loud..........................91

10. Love Anyway.. 103

11. Lingering Goodbyes... 111

12. Own Your Story... 127

13. Girl, Get up 135

About the Author.. 142

FOREWORD

by Joanna Hunt

I met Kristi Caudell at a business coaching event in Palm Beach, Florida, in 2023. We became fast friends—two women of faith navigating the world of business with purpose and grit. At the time, I didn't know much about her personal story. I knew she had been on *The Apprentice* and ran a successful real estate business. She knew I was a book coach and publisher. She told me she wanted to write a book but had no idea where to begin. That's how our professional journey started. But what followed was something unexpected—and so much deeper.

As I got to know Kristi, I was struck by her heart for people. Her passion, tenacity, and business savvy were evident from the start—but it was her resilience that left a lasting impression. What you see with Kristi is what you get: no pretense, no performance. Just a woman who has lived through real life and come out wiser, stronger, and more compassionate on the other side.

In a world obsessed with filters, fillers, and polish, Kristi offers something rare: raw authenticity. Or, as I like to tell her privately—she's badass approachable.

And through the process of writing this book, she lived her message in real time. Kristi faced more challenges and walked through deep personal loss. She said goodbye to her mother—her best friend—and stepped into a new season as an empty nester. And yet, she kept showing up. Page by page, she poured out her story with honesty and courage.

She got up. Again and again.

And so did I.

You see, at the time we met, I was raw and recovering from a deep betrayal by someone I loved—an experience that sent shockwaves through every part of my life. I had no idea that I needed to work with Kristi, just as much as she needed to work with me. As I helped her shape her story, her story helped shape me.

Girl, Get Up isn't just a catchy title—it's a battle cry for every woman who's ever felt knocked down, worn out, discarded, or forgotten. Her words are honest, unfiltered, and fiercely hopeful. Kristi's not just telling her story in this book—she's handing you a lifeline.

I always say: life is a group experience, and healing is a group experience. We aren't meant to go it alone. And if there's anyone qualified to lead the charge, it's Kristi Caudell. If you've ever needed someone to say, "Me too," followed by, "You've got this, let me show you the way," then keep reading.

This book is for you. It's for us.

So clear your calendar for the afternoon, find your comfy chair, and put your feet up. This is a book you won't want to put down—until the end, where I believe you'll find your new beginning.

Don't gloat over me my enemy,
though I have fallen, I will arise . . .
(Micah 7:8).

INTRODUCTION
We're in This Together

Dear Friend,

We've never met before, but I bet we aren't that different.

We've both carried insecurities. We've made mistakes and celebrated victories. We've loved hard and pursued crazy dreams. We've been betrayed. Heartbroken. We've failed—more than once—and probably embarrassed ourselves along the way.

And if you're anything like me, then somewhere along that road, a voice of encouragement made all the difference. Someone's story of getting back up gave you just enough strength to try again.

That's what I hope this book will be for you.

I'm not here with all the answers—I'm here with a story.

A real story. A messy story. A story that's still being written—just like yours.

I don't write from a place of perfection. I write as a fellow traveler—someone who knows what it's like to fall hard and wonder if she can rise again. Someone who's gotten back up with wobbly, skinned knees and a determined heart more times than she can count.

Sometimes we rise strong. Sometimes we rise slow.

But it's one thing to get knocked down. It's another thing entirely when life keeps swinging—and you wonder if you've got anything left.

Have you been there? I have.

Maybe you're there now—standing in a chapter of your life you never saw coming. Feeling tired. Feeling stuck. Feeling like you barely recognize the person you used to be.

Let me tell you something: your feelings and your reality are not always the same.

Your story is not over. No way—it's just getting good.

Let me ask you, in those quiet, predawn hours—when the world is still and the noise falls away—what does your heart whisper?

Do you believe there's more for you?

Do you believe you can rise again?

One thing that has held me steady through the ups and downs of my life is my faith.

That's why this book is called *Girl, Get Up*. It comes from one of my favorite moments in Scripture—in Mark 5:41—where Jesus takes a little girl by the hand, looks right past what everyone else thought was over, and says, *"Little girl, I say to you, get up."*

And she did.

That moment changed her story. And maybe, just maybe, this will be the moment that changes *your* story.

Every time you rise, you rise stronger. Every time you get back up, you're not the same—you're wiser, tougher, more full of grace.

So let's walk this together.

Not perfectly—but boldly.

Not without fear—but anchored in faith.

Not pretending we've got it all figured out, but trusting that God's not done writing our story and that He will work all things together for our good.

So, friend, here's to getting back up.

To standing when it would be easier to stay down.

To becoming who we were always meant to be—one rise at a time.

With love and steadfast belief in your story,

Kristi

CHAPTER 1

Performance Hiding Pain

Before I Learned to Rise, I Had to Survive

Stepping onto the soccer field for the first time as an eighth grader playing junior varsity was intoxicating. The feel of the grass beneath my feet, the weight of the ball at my command—this was more than just a game. It was my first taste of true recognition. Up until that point, my brother had been the athlete everyone cheered for, and I was just a spectator in the stands, desperate to have my moment where *my* efforts, *my* passion, and *my* skill couldn't be ignored.

I've loved soccer for as long as I can remember. In our small town, a girl playing with the boys was unheard of, but no other options existed for me. Dad wasn't too keen on the idea at first. But I persisted. I didn't want to just be included—I wanted to *stand out*. I wanted to prove I wasn't just there to fill a spot but to make a mark. And that's exactly what I did. My dad finally relented and allowed me to join the boys' travel team, marking the beginning of my defiance against the odds and limitations.

With every game, I carved out my place on the field, pushing through every doubt and expectation. The cheers from the crowd fueled me. It was more than recognition for the goals

I scored or the games we won; the cheers were affirmation I was finally seen—not as someone's little sister, not as a girl trying to keep up, but as a competitor in my own right. The applause felt like sunshine breaking through a lifelong overcast sky, and I craved more. But with that light came a shadow I didn't fully understand at the time. I had tied my worth to my performance. Every cheer, every pat on the back, every record set became a piece of the puzzle I desperately tried to complete—a puzzle called *acceptance*. I chased it with everything I had, believing if I could just earn one more nod of approval, I'd finally feel whole.

* * *

If you would have seen me on stage as a high school sophomore at the sports banquet—big smile, red dress, matching shoes, arms full of trophies—you probably would have thought it was the best night of my life. But you'd be wrong.

After the ceremony, my parents left in their car, and I rode home with my brother, Scott. We stayed talking a bit, so we were about thirty minutes behind my parents. Scott is eleven months older than me—my proud big brother—singing my praises all the way home. I floated on the clouds when I walked in the front door and it clicked behind me. There Dad stood in the entry, and before I could even take my shoes off, I knew something was wrong. Not from anything he said but from the look on his face—and the way my mother and brother disappeared out of the room.

I stood across from him for a moment, trying to read the tension. He had that dark, haunting look in his eyes. Growing up, that look was the cue my brother and I should hide in the closet. But this time, he wasn't mad at mom. He looked straight at me.

I tried to smile. "Did you enjoy the banquet, Daddy? Aren't you proud of me?" My voice quivered slightly as I adjusted the trophies in my arms.

See, I was a daddy's girl, his favorite person on the planet. I knew he loved me, and I loved him. He was my biggest champion. But sometimes—sometimes his temper would get the best of him. This night was one of those times.

I couldn't seem to deescalate his palpable anger. Out of nowhere, Daddy shook his head and lunged at me—launching into a verbal and physical tirade.

"How could you be so disrespectful! You embarrass me!" he raged.

"No, Daddy!" I screamed, dropping the trophies and burying my face in my arms. "Please stop!"

He threw my one-hundred-pound frame against the stairs, commanding, "Go to your room!"

I half crawled, half stumbled up the stairs, hoping it was over, but he was just getting started. He charged up the stairs after me, grabbing the hunter-green cordless phone from only God knows where. He chased me to my room and began striking me with it, over and over—his fury materializing with each hit. I curled into a ball, covering my head.

I was in such shock I couldn't speak. When he didn't get the reaction he wanted, it got worse. Before I knew what had happened or why, suddenly he sat on top of me with both hands around my neck.

He gritted the words out through his rage,

"How dare you . . .

. . . chew gum . . .

. . . on stage!"

In terror and desperation, I managed to reach the phone he'd dropped next to me. My survival instinct took over, and I started hitting him as hard as I could. Releasing his grip on me and pulling back, he became more outraged—but somehow, I managed to escape his hold. I ran down the stairs and out the front door, fleeing to my friend Ali's house down the street.

It was over.

Chewing gum.

All of that because I chewed gum on stage.

I was sixteen years old, and that night I learned winning couldn't always keep me safe. Mom never said a word about it. I'd seen her suffer under his abuse, and I knew why she felt so helpless when he was in one of his moods. I also knew why she stayed and loved him so much. It was complicated. We all knew that if we could ride out the hard times, the good times would return. The special bond I shared with my dad wasn't defined by our lowest moments.

* * *

At school the next day, the assistant principal, also my soccer coach's wife, called me into her office. I sat down across from her desk. She lifted my sleeve, examining the marks and bruises.

"Kristi, what happened? Those marks weren't on you at the banquet last night."

"Oh, it's nothing. I fell on the stairs."

I knew she didn't believe me.

I wouldn't have believed me.

She didn't say another word to me and called the

Department of Family and Child Services. I was both humiliated and terrified of what might happen next.

That afternoon, a social worker came to my house. I was smiling and happy, as if I didn't have a care in the world. I would never dare say a negative word about my dad. I knew he didn't mean it, and I didn't want him to get in trouble. After about two hours, the social worker left and never came back.

My dad would eventually apologize—the night of my high

> That night I learned winning couldn't always keep me safe.

school graduation—but I had already forgiven him. Even though there were times growing up when I felt a tangible distance between us—a gap filled with unspoken words and unexpressed feelings—I always sensed a depth of emotion in his eyes, a silent apology he didn't quite know how to voice.

* * *

I was a vivacious young girl, an all-American dreamer growing up in Gainesville, Georgia, with aspirations as vast as the night sky. I was also as southern as they come—never met a stranger and brimming with hopes of conquering the world, one soccer goal at a time. I might not have to tell you I was also raised in a strict home. Christian even. My parents had a lot of rules, but they were for my good. I learned where my strength would eventually come from by watching my mother. She was so full of love and life, teaching me to always forgive, turn the other cheek, and take the high road. My dad taught me to stand up and persevere through adversity. Both of my

5

parents instilled in me the importance of integrity and morality, and I never wanted to disappoint them. Ever.

But there I was, about two months later, sitting in Dr. Martin's office. We were investigating a strange tightness in my abdomen, which I naively thought was an ulcer or even a tumor. He did his initial exam and had me lay back on the table. He squeezed a cold gel onto my belly and pulled out a long medical wand. As soon as it touched me, the machine started pounding.

"What is that?" I asked.

"Well, Kristi, that's your baby's heartbeat. You're about three months pregnant. Maybe four."

I said nothing. *Pregnant?* I couldn't believe my ears! I thought to myself, *I am only sixteen. How is this possible?* I mean, I knew how it was *possible*, but I never imagined one awful night on a mattress on a cold, concrete, basement floor would lead to this life-altering moment. I broke up with my boyfriend a couple of days after it had happened. I was always the girl saving myself for marriage. I knew it. My friends knew it, but in a moment of weakness, I gave away something I could never reclaim. And since I was an athlete, I never had a regular period. I had no clue I was pregnant. It was beyond my comprehension. *Is this for real?* The shock turned to dread as I thought about how my parents would react. My carefully constructed, all-American world slipped through my fingers. I lay there on the table, and as the overwhelm engulfed me, I centered in on the rhythmic whooshing of the tiny heartbeat from the monitor until time stood still.

Dr. Martin called Mom in from the waiting room and broke the news. She was silent. He saw the look on her face and invited us to sit at his desk to talk. This wasn't just any doctor; this was the doctor who had delivered me. He was a family friend, and I played soccer with his son.

"Now, we only have a short amount of time to decide what we're going to do," he said clasping hands on the desk matter-of-factly.

I knew what he meant but *excuse me?*

My thoughts swirled.

Aren't we all Christians? I'm not killing my baby.

A righteous indignation rose up within me.

"What do you mean!?" I said bluntly. "I'm having a baby! That's what *we're* gonna do!" I didn't know much in that moment, but I knew I was having a baby.

And with that, I got up, and Mom and I went to the car.

The appointment was about a month after the incident with my dad, and we were still trying to find our footing. When I did the math in my head, I felt numb realizing I was pregnant when it had happened.

Before the appointment, Mom and I had planned to spend the day together shopping and having girl time. With the news, I wasn't sure what was happening now. I certainly didn't want to go home. I didn't know what to say, but I could feel the weight between us. Mom didn't say a word either. I could feel her processing everything, her quiet presence heavier than usual.

What took me by surprise wasn't just the silence but the fact she didn't turn the car toward home. Instead, she kept driving—straight to the mall. It was always her therapy. We walked into a department store, still not expressing a single word. Then, without hesitation, she headed to the nursery section, stopped, and turned to me, asking, "Boy or girl?"

"Girl," I answered, my voice barely above a whisper. Without missing a beat, she picked out an outfit and bought it.

That moment was profound. In her quiet, unwavering way, my mother showed me exactly who she was. She didn't lecture. She didn't fall apart. She didn't make me feel ashamed. Instead, she showed me love. She showed me support. But most of all, she showed me strength.

* * *

I wasn't so sure about my dad. Breaking the news to my father was one of the hardest moments of my life. I wasn't even sure how to tell him, but after dinner that Friday night, I followed him into the sunroom.

"Dad, I need to talk to you."

"OK, what's up, Champ?" he replied curiously.

I wasn't one to beat around the bush, and neither was he. I sat across from him on the ottoman, looked him in the eye the way he taught, and out it came.

"Dad, we're going to have a baby this Christmas."

He looked puzzled.

"Who's having a baby this Christmas?"

"I am, Daddy. December twenty-fourth."

He said nothing. Not with his words anyway. The look of shock and heartbreak on his face shook me to my core. And then I saw something I had never in my life seen before. My dad's big blue eyes began welling up with tears.

I reached over to him, wrapping my arms around him. "Oh, Daddy!"

Sobs came from his depths, and I just held him as he wept.

"Kristi, I need to be alone for a minute."

He sat back, wiping his face.

"Sure thing, Daddy."

I left him alone in the sunroom and went upstairs. I had always viewed my father as a pillar of strength, a man who faced everything with unwavering resolve. To see him so vulnerable, to witness the raw emotion in his face, was gut-wrenching. It broke something inside of me, but at the same time, it built me up in ways I never expected.

About thirty minutes later I heard his call. "Kristi Lynn! Get down here," he shouted.

I couldn't imagine what was coming. As I approached the sofa, he threw a yellow legal pad with a pen across the top at me, falling to the floor in disarray. I picked it up and sat down. Dad was noticeably upset but also measured and controlled. I could tell his engineer's brain jumped into problem-solving mode.

"Kristi Lynn, you don't realize how damn naïve you are right now and how much this is going to change your life. You've been up on a pedestal, successful and popular. But now, you are going to be seen as low man on the totem pole. There are friends at school whose parents won't want them to hang out with you anymore. People are going whisper behind your back. They are going to look at you differently."

That night, it wasn't just a father talking to his daughter—it was a man who saw me, truly saw me. Not as a child who had made a mistake, but as a young woman about to embark on an unimaginable journey. He knew I needed his help. He never once let disappointment take root. He never yelled or screamed that night, or any night after. He never laid another finger on me ever again. But that night, he challenged me.

"Kristi Lynn, I want you to dig deep and dream bigger than you ever have before. I want you to write down every goal you can think of and look beyond the circumstances you are facing. Now is the time to stretch and go after every dream you ever had."

I immediately started writing down everything just as he instructed:

One: *to be an All-American soccer player.*

Two: *to set athletic records in high school and college, become a nationally ranked player.*

Three: *to buy a home before my child started kindergarten, so she would never feel "different."*

Those goals weren't just words on paper—they became my lifeline. In the face of overwhelming uncertainty, my father's belief in me became the foundation keeping me grounded, the force pushing me to keep moving forward when everything else seemed impossible.

It wasn't just my father's strength carrying me through—it was my mother's quiet, unwavering presence.

She didn't just stand beside me; she walked every step with me. She loved me without question. Without hesitation. Without conditions.

My father's words lit a fire in my heart. But it was my mother's love keeping it burning.

When the weight of the world felt unbearable, she held me.

When I crumbled, she wiped my tears and reminded me I could stand again.

When I doubted my own strength, she never did.

She knew how to love without limits. Without keeping score.

No matter how hard the road became, she was there—

steady and sure—always reminding me I was capable of more than I believed.

Together, my parents gave me the courage to keep going.

My father's tough love and belief in my potential pushed me to dream bigger, reach higher, and set bold goals. My mother's steady love kept me grounded when life felt like too much to carry.

My parents weren't perfect. They didn't have all the answers. There was no playbook for what we were facing.

But they didn't need one.

They just loved me—the best way they knew how.

And that was enough. In fact, it was more than enough.

In doing so, they gave me the greatest gift of all—the foundation to love myself, to trust my own resilience, and to rise above whatever life would throw my way.

CHAPTER 2

Flatlining Dreams

What I Didn't Expect When I Was Expecting

It was July when I found out I was pregnant, and school would be starting soon. After telling my dad, my parents told me I needed to be the one to inform the school. So a couple of weeks later, my mom took me to my coach's house, which was only about two miles away. When I told Coach Childs the news, he was in shock. I assured him I would still be able to play soccer since I wasn't due until the end of December.

The next person I needed to tell was the principal, Mr. Corley. The high school was open, and the staff was in pre-planning for the new school year. My parents drove me to the school, and we walked straight to the principal's office. Mr. Corley was a big man—about 6'4"—and I had to look almost straight up to talk to him.

I stuck my head in his office door.

"Mr. Corley, may I speak to you for a minute?"

"Sure, Kristi, come on in."

I walked in, my parents behind me. I sat down across from his desk in a hunter-green armchair with nail heads. I was ready to rip the Band-Aid off.

"Mr. Corley, I need to tell you something. I'm pregnant."

Mr. Corley was silent. I don't know if he was more shocked by the news or by the way I just laid it out.

He looked at me, then at my dad, and then at my mom.

"Well, is she going to be able to play soccer?"

"Yes, sir!" I answered before my mom could get a word in edgewise.

Then he turned to his computer to print off my schedule.

"Kristi, I'd like for you to go see all of your teachers and let them know. You're going to need to go to the bathroom more than usual . . . and we already know you can't sit still as it is. But this will be a real reason to leave the room."

My parents shook his hand and thanked him. I stood up and right then and there went to go talk to each of my teachers. It was all still so surreal, but from the moment I found out I was pregnant, I just did it. I did what I had to do. I still felt like a normal teenager, and as I looked at my class list, I remember analyzing it like every normal teenager did every normal year.

But little did I know how abnormal this year would be for me.

About a week and a half after school started, I was walking to my next class wearing a long black dress, when another student walked up to me. She looked me up and down, and said, "Kristi, I heard you were pregnant. But now that I see you, I know it's not true."

I half smiled, "No, it is true."

She looked at me in shock.

"OK. Gotta go to class." She was gone.

I didn't have a belly. I didn't look pregnant.

In fact, I never did.

Thursday morning, September 11th, started like any other

morning, but it was the day everything changed. I was getting ready for school, my routine familiar, my thoughts somewhere between the day ahead and the life growing inside me. Then, suddenly, a wave of dizziness hit me. My vision became blurry, and my knees buckled. Before I could make sense of what was happening, the world went dark.

When I came to, I was being helped into a car, my parents' voices urgent but controlled.

"We need to get you to the doctor. Now."

Dad had to go to work, so Mom drove me. Minutes later, we pulled up to my doctor's office at Northeast Georgia Medical Center. Before I could even process where I was, he was already there—Dr. Martin. He wasn't supposed to be there. He was off that day, but he rushed in from his family farm, still in boots and a t-shirt. He took one look at me, then my mom. I saw a look on his face I had never seen before.

"This hospital isn't prepared if you have this baby today or in the near future," he said, his voice calm but firm.

The weight of his words sank deep into my chest.

I was sixteen. I was just a kid. And I was about to have a baby.

It was all a blur. Before I could ask another question, I was in an ambulance headed to Atlanta. It was pouring down rain, and as I sat alone on the gurney with the flashing blue lights all around, I could feel the vehicle occasionally sliding on the slick streets. I'd never ridden that fast in a vehicle before. I wished my mom was with me, but she had to drive her car down to Atlanta. I clutched my belly the entire way, whispering silent prayers, trying to convince myself everything was going to be OK.

That I wasn't too young.

That this baby wasn't too small.

That God wasn't going to take her from me before I ever got the chance to hold her.

When I arrived in Atlanta, they stabilized me and the baby. I learned I had a serious condition called preeclampsia toxemia, which can be fatal for both mother and baby.

Three days passed in a haze—machines beeping, nurses checking vitals constantly, doctors monitoring every move. The panic of that first day had settled just enough for everyone to breathe again, even if only slightly. They moved me from the ICU to a regular room. Dad brought me movies and set up a VHS player and Nintendo, which I thought was sweet. I barely played Nintendo unless it was Wheel of Fortune with Ali.

It was now Saturday night, and I convinced my parents to go home and get some rest. They had been by my side every moment, and I saw exhaustion heavy in their eyes. I felt comforted by the staff and had a favorite nurse, Tracy, so I told them, "I'm OK. Go home. Sleep. I'll call if anything changes."

I believed it when I said it.

But I was wrong.

That night, everything unraveled.

I woke in the night with a tightness in my chest—subtle at first, like someone pressing down lightly. Then it got worse. Much worse.

I couldn't breathe.

I gasped for air, but it felt like I was drowning. My lungs wouldn't fill. My body was betraying me.

"I can't breathe," I whispered to the nurse.

She checked the monitors, adjusted my bed, and reassured me.

"It's just some indigestion," she said gently.

The hours crawled by. I struggled through every minute. No matter how I positioned myself, no matter how deeply I tried to inhale, the air just wouldn't come. I was suffocating in my own body.

The next morning, the doctor came by on his rounds. When he saw me, I saw that same panic in his face again. He didn't ask how I was feeling—he could see it. My pale skin, the erratic monitor readings, the shallow rise and fall of my chest. Not only that, I think I doubled in size overnight.

> Sometimes the miracle isn't in the rescue; it's in the endurance.

And then—chaos.

"Prep her for surgery. We're taking this baby today."

Everything happened at once. Nurses rushed in. Hands pulled wires, adjusted IVs, moved monitors. Voices blurred together.

I was sixteen years old. And in a matter of minutes, I would no longer be just a child. I would be a mother. But yet, I needed my mother.

I called for Tracy, the one nurse I trusted most. I was terrified. In less than a minute, she was by my side. She grabbed my hand, her voice steady while mine trembled.

She called my parents. They didn't know what was happening. And I was so scared.

Tracy stayed with me, held my hand, and whispered reassurance as my world spun out of control. "I won't leave you," she promised. "Not until your mom and dad get here."

I clung to her words like a lifeline. For those terrifying minutes before my parents arrived, she was all I had.

I was rushed down the hallway, wheels of the hospital bed rattling beneath me, fluorescent lights flickering above.

My heart pounded, fear coursing through my veins.

The operating room was a blur of sterile blue and harsh white light. I was wheeled in, my body both heavy and weightless at the same time. Machines were beeping. Voices overlapping.

I could feel everything.

The first epidural didn't work. Neither did the second. The fluid buildup stretched my skin tight. My fingers were unrecognizable—swollen beyond anything I'd ever seen.

Finally, the numbness spread.

A moment of relief. Just for a second.

Somewhere in the chaos, my mother arrived. Tracy had kept her promise and stayed with me until she got there. Turning to my mother, I searched her face for strength, for reassurance. For anything.

I was scared to death.

Mom looked at my hand, then into my eyes. She placed her hand gently over mine.

"It's OK, baby. It's OK. Everything is going to be OK."

She said the words, but in her eyes, I saw something different.

As terrified as I was of losing my baby, she was of losing hers.

The nurses placed three five-gallon buckets on the floor beside me. As the doctor installed the drains, I begged them to put me to sleep. They wouldn't. I just stared up at the ceiling as the doctors moved around me, their voices now just white noise.

A mask was placed over my nose, a cool sensation washing

over my face. My limbs felt as if they were floating. I focused on my mother's grip, the warmth of her hand—my only anchor.

Then everything faded.

The darkness swallowed me whole.

For a moment—maybe a second, maybe an eternity—there was nothing.

No sound. No pain. Just a weightless void.

Chaos erupted again.

The scalpel touched my skin and a surge of fluid gushed—gallons of it—poured from my body. One bucket, then two, then three. But the worst of it wasn't visible.

The fluid had surrounded my heart.

My body was shutting down. Drowning from the inside.

Then came the words that sliced through the room like a blade.

"We're losing her."

The anesthetist's voice was tight, cracking beneath the moment. Again, she said it with slightly more intensity, "We're losing her!"

My parents had already communicated their wishes to the medical team: if it came down to making a choice, they were to save me.

Now the focus shifted—from my precious baby to *their* baby. I was dying on the table.

Suddenly, my mother's hand—my anchor—was ripped away. I watched the back of her head disappear in a blur as she was rushed out of the room.

"Clear!"

The paddles hit my chest.

A jolt of electricity surged through me.

And then it went dark.

* * *

I was in a coma for three days.

While I was out, I could hear people around me talking about "the baby," but I couldn't grasp what was being said. When I was fully asleep, I had unusually vivid dreams. In one, I was playing soccer on the most beautiful field I'd ever seen— lush, bright-green grass surrounded by a canopy of trees. I scored the winning goal and felt the sunshine on my face and the joy of sweet victory. In another dream, I had two babies— Catelyn and Callie. I thought something happened to Callie and that she had died. I freaked out in my unconscious state, desperate to wake myself up. But I couldn't.

Finally, the day came when I opened my eyes to the familiar beeping sounds of a hospital room. The bright light streaming through the window practically blinded me. My parents were there, but before they noticed I was awake, I mumbled, "What happened to the other baby?"

They both rushed to my side.

"What happened to the other baby?" I asked again, more clearly.

My mom showed me polaroids of a tiny baby in an incubator in the NICU. She was gorgeous. I held those photos in my hands, just staring at them—snapshots of a miniature warrior. Her head was the size of a tennis ball—so delicate, so perfect, so impossibly small.

I had so much to say, but I barely had the strength to speak.

My daughter entered the world against impossible odds. She weighed just two pounds, two ounces at birth—so small, so fragile. Over the next few days, she dropped to one pound, eight ounces. Her body was barely more than a whisper. Yet, against all expectations, she was strong. She didn't need transfusions. She didn't need surgeries. She breathed on her own within forty-eight hours. It was unheard of.

She was nothing short of a miracle. A miracle baby.

I named her Catelyn—just like in my dream. And I spelled it exactly the way I saw it too.

As it turned out, there wasn't a second baby. But in my stupor, I had been so certain there was I made the doctors show me the medical records!

Finally, the moment came where I could see her. The nurse wheeled me down to the NICU, Mom by my side, the sterile scent of the hospital thick in the air and my heart pounding in anticipation.

I scrubbed in before entering the NICU, and all the way in the very back there she was.

I felt breathless.

So tiny, tucked inside the incubator. Too small to hold. Covered in wires. Surrounded by machines humming softly around her. But none of that mattered.

She was here.

I didn't see the tubes. I didn't see the medical equipment. I only saw her.

I looked at her—this impossibly small, determined little fighter—and the world outside faded. It was just us.

We both survived.

And if we survived that, we could survive anything.

In that moment, I made a silent vow:

It's you and me against the world, baby girl. So, watch out world!

We wouldn't just live—we would live *fully*. Every single day.

* * *

I stayed in the hospital for three weeks. By the time I was discharged, I no longer had cardiomyopathy. Eventually, Catelyn was transferred to Northeast Georgia Medical Center, just fifteen minutes from home instead of an hour and a half away.

I was six weeks post-partum when Coach Sam called my parents and asked if I could play in the soccer game the next Sunday. The team needed me, but more importantly, I needed to get back on the field. I remember sitting on my knees in front of my father sitting in his chair begging, "Please, let me go play! Please!" And so he did. That Sunday I was both thrilled to play and terrified to be hit in the stomach being six weeks after a C-section. But of the three goals scored that day I scored two, and we won the game.

* * *

The day finally came when Catelyn gained enough weight to come home. She needed to weigh at least four and a half pounds to ride in the car seat, and she reached that milestone on November 5, 1997. Most preemies don't come home until their due date, which hers wasn't until the end of December. She beat all the odds—another prime example of the strength in my precious blonde-haired, blue-eyed fighter.

Coming home, she wore a preemie dress my mom bought for her, and to honor tradition, she wore the same handmade sweater and bonnet I had worn home from the hospital. Mom thought of that, and I loved it. I loaded her up in her car seat to finally take her home.

My dad's heart had softened over those weeks. When I pulled up in the driveway with her, he came running out the door holding a porcelain plate that read "Welcome Home Catelyn Victoria 9-14-97." Sweet music played inside, and there were snacks on the counter. It was the perfect homecoming.

Catelyn was still on a heart monitor, and we had to keep her room at a specific temperature while her body acclimated to her new world. She didn't arrive home to a long-awaited nursery; I only knew I was pregnant for about two months! But my mom and dad transformed the downstairs guest room into a space for me and Catelyn. They set up a twin bed, a crib, and a bassinet. One of my mom's best friends even made a beautiful skirt for the bassinet. It was perfect.

Since I couldn't return to school, I was placed on "hospital homebound." My coach—Coach Childs—was also my assigned homebound teacher. He had a lot of mercy and compassion for me and my situation. He would bring me a copy of a test ahead of time and say, "Here, study this."

* * *

And that's how the next chapter of our story began—me and my miracle girl—at home, alive, together, and already beating the odds. We didn't have everything figured out, but we had each other. And that was more than enough. I was no longer just a teenager. I was a mother. A fighter. A survivor. And from that moment on I knew one thing was for sure—God doesn't always calm the storm. Sometimes,

He lets the wind howl and the waves crash so we'll learn to rise above it.

Catelyn wasn't just my baby; she was my "why." In saving her life, in many ways she saved mine too.

Maybe you're facing a storm of your own, wondering how you'll make it through. Maybe you're exhausted, stretched thin, or quietly drowning under the weight of it all. I see you. And I need you to know something: You are stronger than you think.

The breaking you feel right now is not the end of your story—

It's the beginning of your becoming.

Sometimes, the miracle isn't in the rescue, it's in the endurance. Sometimes, the victory isn't obvious—but it's in the fact that you're still standing. Still fighting. Still showing up. That's not weakness. That's warrior-level strength!

So take a breath. Wipe your tears and keep going. Keep going because your story isn't over and your miracle might be just on the other side of the pain. Remember, you were born to rise.

CHAPTER 3

Cleats to the Fire

Post Trauma...but Not Post Struggle

Before returning to school, mom made a few phone calls looking for referrals of someone who could keep Catelyn in their home. I needed a safe place for my precious baby, someone I could trust, and that's what led us to Miss Pam.

I still remember that day like it was yesterday. Catelyn was buckled in her little white car seat with navy fabric and tiny red flowers. She was still tethered to her heart monitor, fragile and small but full of life. And Miss Pam—well, she couldn't wait to get her hands on Catelyn. The moment we arrived, we were welcomed by her loving eyes. She scooped Catelyn up as if she had been waiting her whole life to love her. From that day, Miss Pam became a steady presence in our lives. Catelyn stayed with her all the way through pre-K. She wasn't just a babysitter. She was a lifeline—the kind of woman who loved deeply, served quietly, and nurtured with grace.

This was one of those moments when God showed up and met the need before I even knew how to pray for it. Miss Pam was part of a village that raised my daughter, and she'll forever be part of our story.

* * *

Going back to high school as a young, single mom, I felt the weight of the world's judgment pressing down on me. I was previously well liked in school and friendly with everyone. I talked to everybody and didn't get into cliques; although, most of my friends were athletes because I was one myself. At one point I was co-captain of the cheerleading squad and later became captain of my soccer team, so I naturally ran with that crowd. Things were different now. I tried to seamlessly fit back into my friend group, but it wasn't so seamless. Here I was, sixteen years old with a car seat in the back of my car. The whispers, the stares—they all seemed to say: *You don't fit in. You're a loser. You'll never make it.* There were parties and meet ups at Wahoo Creek Park I was never invited to and couldn't attend anyway. My life was so incredibly different from all the other students. I had a baby to go home to.

One day, I sat at lunch with a group of friends. Tiffany, who was on the cheerleading squad, noticed a pregnant classmate walking by. She had a big ol' belly and was probably close to her due date. When I was pregnant, I never showed, so many people didn't even see me "that way."

Tiffany's eyes darted up and down at the girl with a look of disgust. She leaned in and said to our group, "It's so embarrassing having all these pregnant girls in our school." That sent my blood boiling, and I could feel a fire welling up within me.

I looked straight at her and said, "Well, we have way more bitches in this school than we will ever have pregnant girls." With that I got up, grabbed my lunch tray, and walked over to sit with the other teen moms.

The pressure wasn't just at school. Everywhere I went there were stares and whispers. I was walking into Target one day and a woman on her way out nearly broke her neck glaring at me as she passed. You'd have thought I had three heads! It was more than a glare—it was a message. She wanted me to see her, and she wanted me to feel her disapproval. Believe me, I got the message loud and clear. But I didn't take it personally.

Instead, I thought, "I wonder what skeletons she has in her closet that she has to project such hate and judgement onto me."

Even still, I tried to be a normal teenager as much as possible. I attended as many school functions as I could, baby in tow oftentimes. One day I was in the stands at a Gainesville High School baseball game. Jason Smith was up to bat. He was the cutest boy in school, tall, blonde, and every girl in three counties wanted to date him. I was also enamored with him, but he didn't even know I existed. *I'll never get a guy like that*, I thought to myself.

* * *

My sense of purpose at school made a shift one day when the counselor called me into her office. She wanted me to meet another young pregnant lady who didn't have any support. In fact, the more I got to know the other teen moms in the school, the more I became aware most of them didn't have a support network or resources like I did.

One day, I went home and talked to my mom about what we could do. We decided to start a group for teen moms. The school counselor would facilitate and a social worker would come to lead weekly meetings in the library and share from the book *What to Expect When You're Expecting*. We took donations and partnered with community organizations to get the resources these young girls needed. I was happy to be in a position to help and even more grateful for the support I had.

* * *

For the rest of my school life, soccer was my escape. On the field, I wasn't *the girl who had a baby at sixteen* or *the girl constantly trying to prove herself*. I was a force to be reckoned with, and my coaches saw it before I ever did. They trained me, pushed me, and supported me in ways that carried me through the toughest seasons of my life. And I ran with it—literally. Every grueling sprint, every after-practice penalty shot, every bead of sweat and aching muscle was proof that I was still standing, still fighting, and still proving that being underestimated was my greatest weapon. By ninth grade, I played varsity. I set records in high school that still haven't been broken, and when I moved on to the college level, I became a nationally ranked scorer and an All-American nominee. Those weren't just titles—they were affirmations all my effort, all my struggles, had led to something tangible.

* * *

It was the end of my senior year, and during the week leading up to graduation, the seniors were honored and recognized for their accomplishments at an event called Senior Night. Held at the football stadium, when called, each student would walk out onto the field and listen as the announcer read all their accolades. When it was my turn, Dad escorted me onto the field, and we stood there longer than anyone else that night as they announced award after award. As I looked out to the crowd absorbing the familiar applause, standing arm in arm with my dad, he leaned over and said to me, "Champ, you're back." A sense of relief rushed over me. My dad was proud of me, and I knew I was going to be alright.

Graduation was a night I will never forget. I wasn't sure if my dad was going to make it to the ceremony because he traveled so much for work. We never talked about it. I had just become accustomed to not knowing when he would

> Maybe the breakthrough comes—not in spite of the chaos, but because of it.

be around or not. After the ceremony, I walked out to the lobby of the Georgia Mountain Center when my mom and dad walked up to me. He had a small gift in his hand. I was shocked. Mom always did the gift giving, but this was something *from him*. I opened the small gold box, and there was a charm bracelet inside. It had a '99, a soccer ball, and some other charms to mark the milestones of my life up to that point. But what meant the most was the note he placed inside. My dad had the most beautiful handwriting, the simple words struck deep into my heart: *I'm sorry. Love Dad.*

* * *

I had a full-ride soccer scholarship to more than one school. My coaches and I had worked so hard cutting out newspaper clippings of me playing in high school and sending them out to the colleges. Young Harris College was number one in soccer at the time, and that's where I had my sights set. It was about an hour from home, so it made perfect sense for me to attend there.

As a single mom, I couldn't stay at the dorm, but I received enough scholarship money to cover my housing. I was all in and ready to commit. The coach was extremely supportive of me as well being a teenage mother. However, my dad had gone to Truett McConnell Baptist College, and as we drove home from visiting Harris College, he said, "Let's just stop by Truett and take a look. It's on the way anyway." I had no intention of changing my mind. Truett didn't even have an impressive soccer program, but to make Daddy happy, I agreed to stop by and just look.

When we finally arrived at Truett, Dad drove straight to the soccer field. As we came closer, I couldn't believe what my eyes saw. As I looked out, I was completely overwhelmed with emotion. Before he could even finish putting his white Jeep Cherokee in park, I jumped out and ran to the grass. It felt like walking on clouds.

This was it.

This was *really* it!

I turned around, and Dad has his hands in his front pockets leaning up against his Jeep with a smile. I looked back at the field. *The* field. Lush green grass and tall, towering trees. It was unlike any place I had ever seen before—in person. But I had seen this place in my dream when Catelyn was born. This was exactly where I was supposed to be.

Coach Childs hadn't been with Truett long when our paths crossed again. He had just taken the job as the new women's soccer coach, stepping into a role that truthfully didn't come with much—no real program to speak of, barely enough players to fill the team, and zero wins under his belt. It was a program still waiting for a story to be written. But that was all about to change.

Coach Childs actually recruited me back when I was still in high school. At the time, I knew Truett didn't have a solid program, and as much as I respected him because he was the son of my current high school coach, I just wasn't sure if Truett was the right fit for me. Eventually, I made the decision to play for him, and let me tell you—what unfolded on the field was nothing short of unforgettable. Coach stretched me in ways that still resonate with me today.

At practice when we would run the cross-country track, he would let all of the other girls go ahead of me, calling them name by name, and then he would run ahead of me through the trees. I would hear him say, "Kristi, go."

I would sprint past every player asking if there was anyone in front of them until I reached the front and came in first. He knew exactly what he was doing! Then, after practice, I would stay and shoot one hundred penalty kicks. My coaches could not have been better. They allowed me to bring Catelyn to practice and even had her little soccer balls to play with.

Game after game, win after win, we became a force. Coach Childs didn't just build a program; he built a culture, a family of gritty, determined women who refused to settle—some of the most amazing teammates I've ever had the chance to play with. Coach Childs led us with heart, humility, and a quiet confidence making you want to give him everything you had. I always brought everything I had to the field when I played.

Coach Childs wasn't just coaching us to win games, he was shaping young women for life; teaching us about leadership, perseverance, the power of belief, and what's possible even when no one else sees it yet. What started as an uncertain decision turned into one of the greatest seasons of my life. And it all began with a coach who saw potential where others saw nothing and a team that proved together we could be something great. The first year we came in second, and our second year, we came in first.

* * *

When I was in high school and college, over the summers I earned money as a beverage cart girl at the golf course and worked the gas docks at Gainesville Marina. I continued working as a beverage cart girl over the summer throughout college. After college, I took a job in sales for an IT company through a connection my brother had. I quickly became successful in sales but also became a target. The other salespeople became jealous of my success. But the CEO saw potential in me and became my first mentor. I learned so much from him. Sadly, he passed about six months later, and I was let go by the VP who stepped into his role.

It was a lot to process, but I still had my job at the golf course on the weekends, or so I thought. The next week I walked in to look at my schedule posted in the back office, and for the first time I couldn't find my name listed. My manager said, "Kristi, Mr. Loughlin wants to see you in the conference center."

Well hell, I thought.

I couldn't imagine what was going on at this point.

I pushed open the door to the conference center. "Hi, Mr. Loughlin, you wanted to see me."

"Hey, kid, come on in."

"Do you know why I'm not on the schedule?" I asked.

"Well, you don't work up there anymore; you work with me now."

"I do? Doing what?"

"We've gotta turn this golf course around. So we can sell it."

"OK."

And that's how I got into "fix and flips" and really learned about business and real estate. I started working with one of the investors Mr. Loughlin brought in on the project, Bob Tablak. Bob would become by most favorite boss and mentored me in all things business and taught me how to value myself. One day he said to me, "Kristi, you need to ask for a raise."

"I do?"

"Yes, I'm going to coach you on how to do it."

He spent the next forty-five minutes coaching me on how to ask for a raise, so then I went home and structured my presentation. The next day I was ready. I walked into his office with my presentation on an 8x14 piece of paper. He laughed when I presented it. I asked for double my current salary, which he declined, although he still gave me a good raise. I have no doubt he was extremely proud of the ask.

Bob also taught me to dream. He was constantly pushing me to think bigger and go outside the box. He used to tell me, "Kristi, you know I'm going to be the last person you ever work for."

He was right. Bob is now an advisor for one of my companies, and I don't make too many major moves in life without discussing it with him first.

* * *

After college, I was back living at home. One morning while drying my hair, Dad came in and said, "We're going to look at houses this weekend."

"We are? Where are you going to look?" I asked.

"Well, where do *you* want to live?"

I thought he meant he and mom were looking at houses, but he was taking *me* to go look for a place of my own. This was the last goal on the list I made the night I told Dad I was pregnant.

That weekend, we started driving around and looking at what was on the market, and I just didn't see anything I liked. But after a couple of hours, I saw some cute little townhouses in a row on my left. This one was tan stucco, with black shutters and a black door with glass panes, a cute little green wreath, and two large urns on either side. "Look, Daddy, those are so cute!"

My dad turned left on Forrest Ave and parked right outside the one I liked the best. "Kristi, go knock on the door and ask them if they want to sell their house."

"What? I can't do that!" I was only twenty-two. I was bold, but that was *really bold*.

"Well, I'll just sit here until you do. I have all day."

I knew he meant it. So I nervously walked to the door and knocked. A lovely woman answered. She looked familiar.

"Hi there. I'm Kristi. My Dad and I are just out looking at houses. Have you ever thought about selling your house?"

"Well, honey, we were just now talking about that! You wanna come in?" I peeked inside and the interior was fabulous! I motioned over to Dad to come in, and sure enough—we all knew each other. Susan Mittchell was my Sunday School teacher when I was around five years old. She remembered vividly because I was the "spirited" child of the class. She was

34

also an interior designer, and I loved every inch of that house. Within weeks we closed on that property, and I got to cross "owning a home before Catelyn started kindergarten" off my goal list.

One night, I was invited to a pool party at a friend's house. They were good family friends, and in fact, Mom, Dad, and Catelyn were on vacation in 30A at their condo on the beach in Florida. So I stopped over at the party by myself after work. I was wearing a yellow polo shirt and baby blue shorts. I walked in the door. I was greeted by a friend, Sarah, and off to the kitchen we went. As I walked into the kitchen, there he was—Jason Smith. He was as gorgeous as I remembered, and I immediately felt butterflies. I grabbed a cup to pour a drink, and he walked over to me and introduced himself. We started chatting that night and developed a friendship that became a courtship and then an engagement. Jason didn't date much in high school, and I became his first love. I couldn't believe it. Me—the single mom who was shunned through school got the guy everybody else wanted.

I could finally begin to see how every step, every setback, every unlikely connection was part of a much bigger plan. From the moment Miss Pam scooped sweet little precious Catelyn into her arms to the final whistle on that soccer field; from late-night diaper changes to late-night study sessions and bold prayers, God was shaping something in me I couldn't yet see. He was writing a story of redemption, resilience, and relentless hope. I didn't always feel ready. I didn't always feel seen. But somehow, I kept showing up. And every time I thought I'd reached the end of what I could handle, I found another level of strength waiting on the other side.

Maybe that's how it works for all of us. Maybe the

breakthrough comes not in spite of the chaos but because of it.

So if you're in the thick of it right now—unsure, unseen, underestimated—I want you to know this: your story isn't finished. You're being prepared for more than you can imagine, so keep going because the next chapter might just be the one that changes everything.

* * *

She is clothed with strength and dignity,
and she laughs without fear of the future
(Proverbs 31:25).

CHAPTER 4

Trumping Reality

When There Was no Script, I Wrote My Own

As a twenty-four-year-old woman I was driven by goals and ambition, intensely focused as a single mom. I didn't have time for distractions, like television or a social life outside of my fiancé and family. The only show I ever watched was *The Apprentice*.

One morning my mom called me. "Kristi, *The Apprentice* is coming to Atlanta for a casting call. You need to go!" At first, I completely shrugged it off. *No way.* I was living a carefully crafted life where I made sure every goal I set was attainable. This didn't seem attainable. But my mom persisted as always. She stayed after me all day, reminding me of all the things she had done for me, and finally, she said, "Kristi. Please. Do this *for me.*" It was a low blow, but it worked. So with a mixture of reluctance and excitement, I agreed—for mom.

It was a Thursday, and the casting call was that Saturday at 9:00 a.m. First and foremost, I needed the perfect outfit, so Mom and I went shopping of course. I figured most people would be in dark suits, and I wanted to stand out, so I bought a white suit and chose a pink shirt to go under it. The next afternoon, I packed my suit in my little bag and drove an hour to Atlanta to get in line. It was about 5:00 p.m. on Friday when I arrived. I was second in line. All throughout the night, the line got longer and longer, wrapping around the building. Hundreds if not thousands gathered. News stations came and interviewed us. When all was said and done, it was reported that over a million people applied for that season. Around 8:00 a.m. Saturday, I got my ticket to be in the first group of ten people to be interviewed. I had just enough time to change my clothes and freshen up. I was tired, excited, and nervous, but I knew I always performed my best under pressure.

At 9:00 a.m. our group was called. We walked into one of the hotel ballrooms, and there was a large U-shaped table with a man sitting at the head of it. In a flash I sized him up. He had a drink in his right hand, which signaled he was right-side dominant, so I walked straight over and sat to his right.

"Welcome, everyone. I'm going to ask a question, and I want you all to answer at the same time. Don't worry; I'll be able to hear all of you." You could see the puzzled faces all across the room, but there certainly wasn't time to object. The interviewer asked the open-ended question and everyone started talking. It seemed like sheer chaos. The interviewer looked straight ahead, and I raised my voice in hopes of getting his attention.

Then I turned to him and said, "Excuse me; I need you to listen with your face." I motioned for him to look at me. His expression was a mix of shock and intrigue . . . like "Dayamn!" as we would say in the South.

After all the questions were asked and answered, we were dismissed and told we would get a call that night if we were chosen for a one-on-one interview the next day. As I walked out of the building and looked down at the endless line, I was so grateful I wasn't waiting in the sun all day. I also learned later that being first meant we got twenty minutes of inter-view time, whereas the rest of the groups were ten minutes or less.

At this point, I wanted to win. Badly. As I drove home, I called my parents, who were watching seven-year-old Catelyn for me. I asked them to keep her the rest of the day because I would either need to prepare for an interview or cry. Either way I needed to be alone.

I spent the afternoon trying to relax, and around 6:00 p.m. the phone rang. My heart fluttered as I answered the phone. It was the callback. I got it! I hung up and immediately dialed my parents.

My dad said, "Kristi Lynn, I'll be right over. We're going to prepare together." In minutes he was there coaching me and roleplaying for the next two hours. We reviewed a good handshake, the basics of negotiations, and how to keep eye contact—one of the most effective power tactics of all.

The next day, I drove back to Atlanta. This time I wore black, my staple. Not a suit but business attire. They did a one-on-one interview on camera. If you couldn't perform on camera, there was no advancing. At the end of that round, they again told me they would be in touch if I was selected.

That night, the phone rang again. This time they were sending me a huge packet to fill out. They wanted to know everything about me, my friends, my background, references, businesses, etc. When I say everything, I mean everything—it was like applying for top secret security clearance. After about a week of sitting on pins and needles, I got an email inviting me to LA for a week for the next round of interviews.

In LA, things were very different. Once I arrived at the hotel, I wasn't allowed to talk to anyone. Not even the staff.

I didn't know who around me was there for an interview or anything else. I was assigned a person; Caitlyn was her name, ironically. She was a Burnett staff member who would escort me anywhere I wanted to go. If I wanted to go eat, I had to be escorted; if I wanted to work out, I had to be escorted. Anytime I left my room for any reason, I had to call Caitlyn. She escorted me to various meetings and interviews all week. I had a physical assessment; I had to meet with a psychologist, and I had some really intense interviews. It was like business boot camp! Each morning when we went down for breakfast, there were less and less people in the dining room. Finally, I had an interview with Mark Burnett and J Beinstock. I was so exhausted by that time, and I had been pushed all week. I barely remember what happened; I just walked out feeling like I really didn't do my best.

As Caitlyn walked me back to my room, she said to me, "Kristi, I want to give you some feedback. Tomorrow is the last interview, and you've really got to bring you're A-game. I mean really bring it. This is where it all counts."

That night in my room, I couldn't relax. My mind raced, my emotions all over the place. In moments like this, I pull back from the world—not because I don't have people to call but because I need to silence the outside noise. I needed to hear my own voice to steady myself. So I paced the floor, then stared at my reflection in the mirror, and gave myself the pep talk of my life.

The next morning, I felt ready. Caitlyn came to escort me to breakfast and back. I was supposed to be ready by 11:00 a.m., and I had plenty of time. But as I got out of the shower, I heard pounding at my door. I quickly wrapped myself in a towel and realized it was Caitlyn.

"Kristi, we gotta go now! Right now! Hurry!" As I opened the door, she barged in and started pulling clothes out of my closet. "Here, put this on! Let's go!" I grabbed mascara at least and turned the hair dryer on for thirty seconds, but it didn't help. We ran to the elevator, and she said, "Kristi, this is it. You gotta bring it."

I looked at her and said, "He's here, isn't he? Trump is here." She didn't confirm or deny. Oddly enough, a sense of confidence rushed over me. I knew the higher the stakes, the better I would do.

> Life isn't about proving yourself, it's about living.

The elevator doors opened, and there were the rest of the contestants, maybe ten to twenty people, some with wet hair like me. We headed toward a set of double doors, and I made sure to be the first in line. I wanted a clear assessment of the room as soon as the doors opened. I vividly remember the clicking of the doors and seeing Donald Trump across the room for the first time wearing his iconic red tie, with about ten people lined up on either side. I walked straight toward him with a big smile, making eye contact as my dad taught. Our eyes locked. I sat right across from him without breaking contact, and now we were in a staring contest. It was as if the rest of the room didn't exist. People were coming in and getting seated. No one said a word. All eyes were on us.

Mr. Trump leaned forward. I leaned forward.

Mark Barnett broke the awkward silence. "Confidence. I love a confident woman."

"She's intimidated," Mr. Trump said without a blink.

"Absolutely not!" I laughed at the absurdity. "I'm just

excited to be here. We are both human; we are just in different places in life."

"You're the soccer player from Georgia, aren't you?" He clearly had done his homework.

"Yes, sir."

I'd always been proud of my roots and my athletic background, and it seemed Mr. Trump was someone who valued athletes. I later learned he had a special appreciation for people who had the drive and discipline sports instilled in them. And what stood out to me was how he genuinely cared about seeing people succeed.

As he talked about how he loved hiring athletes, and why, other people started chiming into the conversation, vying for "airtime" with him. It evolved into a group discussion, sharing about our backgrounds, experience, and interests. At one point, another applicant started heckling me and trying to marginalize me. "Oh *she* just went to some state college. I went to Wharton." He bragged about attending Trump's alma mater.

His words triggered my insecurities, and I'm sure you could see them all over my face. Mr. Trump took one look at me and turned to him and said, "That's enough. You needed Wharton; she didn't."

After about an hour, they released us back to our rooms. I just sat in my room, mind racing. *I just met Donald Trump! And we liked each other!* Despite the intensity of the interview process, I couldn't shake the connection we had. Trump's energy was magnetic, his presence commanding, but there was also a certain grace in how he led. I saw firsthand how he could adjust his tone—switching from casual conversation to business mode in an instant. His ability to bring people together for the greater good, even amidst tension, was something that marked me for years.

That evening, Caitlyn came back to my room and said, "Let's go. You are going to meet with Burnett and Beinstock one last time." I stirred up all the strength I had left for one final interview.

At the end of the interview, Mark said, "Well, congratulations; you made it onto the show."

The range of emotion I felt in that moment was indescribable. It was all so surreal. I thought, *Holy shit, I did it!* I never thought it was attainable. From spending the night on the street just to be the first in line for the casting call to countless interviews to the psychological evaluations, everything was designed to test us—to see if we could handle the pressure. But nothing could have prepared me for what was about to come.

The next morning, I flew home, but I could tell no one about my experience. My family, who knew I would be gone for eight weeks, had to sign a nondisclosure agreement with a penalty of a million dollars if they said anything. As it happened, right before filming, I was wrapping up the sale of a hotel and golf course and had planned to take a few weeks off anyway so the timing of the show worked out perfectly. The only thing I had going on during that period was my wedding—which I postponed.

I had just a few weeks to get ready to leave for New York, and it flew by. The crew came and filmed at my home and business. We strategically had made up a story about why a camera crew was there to not give anything away. I barely had time to prepare or even pack. I was told to bring teal accents for the show, and I could only take two suitcases. I flew to

New York by myself and arrived at Korman Communities in Manhattan on 42nd between second and third. Week one was press week, and I had my own apartment until we started filming. The contestants all gathered for various promotions, but we weren't allowed to talk to each other. Even still, I could read people's body language and picked up their attitudes and energy. One of the contestants, Felicia, and I vibed before we could ever talk.

After the first week, we all got transferred to Trump Towers to a single shared apartment and had zero privacy. There were cameras and mics everywhere. The walls didn't even go all the way up to the ceiling. We were all so excited though. We didn't even care, and our collective energy was through the roof.

The first day of filming, we were on lockdown, not allowed to speak until the cameras were rolling. We were picked up from Korman Communities in a couple of large SUVs and driven out to Trump International Golf Course for the first challenge. Donald Trump arrived and divided us into two teams, men against the women. The challenge was to raise money by selling a fitness class at Balley's Total Fitness. Fitness was right up my alley, so even though I swore to myself I wouldn't be the project manager, here I was, the first project manager.

Mr. Trump offered his helicopter to the team who could find where it was parked on the course first. Everyone took off running, but needless to say, my heels did not allow me to showcase my speed. Chris Valletta won the ride back to the city, and his team got to choose the location to do the challenge. He chose Manhattan, while me and my team were placed in the Bronx.

We had twenty-four hours to create a workout class,

market it, and sell it. By this time, I was already existing on Red Bulls and granola bars. To make a long story short, my team lost by eleven dollars. Eleven dollars . . . and I was in the Bronx while they were in the city. However, we had the better ROI, so I argued that position in the boardroom. It wasn't enough; although, Mr. Trump appreciated my business acumen. The time came for me to choose two people to come back to the boardroom with, but in my mind, it was clear who needed to be fired. There was one person who was negative, critical, and judgmental the entire day.

I said, "Mr. Trump, I'm going to make this easy for you. I'm only going to bring back the person you need to fire."

He said, "That's probably not very smart, but sure."

It was a risky move for me, but I couldn't honestly point to anyone else for the loss. Here I was, my first day on the show, and against my better judgement, I was the first project manager, the first loss, and the first one in the boardroom. It was a grueling experience to say the least. At the end of the day, thankfully he fired Melissa. She, herself, admitted she couldn't work well with other women, so she sealed her own fate.

The walk back to the suite was completely surreal. I felt like I had escaped death! I opened the door, and the whole room erupted when they saw me.

The next couple of episodes I found my rhythm and made allies. However, by

episode five, I was back in the boardroom—it was the "Zathura" episode—ironically titled "Lost in Space"—and under Jennifer Murphy's leadership, our team, Capital Edge, struggled from the start. The task seemed simple: design a parade float that would capture the adventure and excitement of the upcoming film. But execution? That was another story.

From the beginning, there were inconsistencies—issues with scaling, design flaws, a lack of a cohesive vision. And then there was the pitch. Oh, the pitch. Jennifer mispronounced the film's title not once, not twice, but over and over again—"Zethura." We all cringed with every repetition, the moment stretching into something almost unbearable. I could see the executives' faces shift from polite interest to quiet mortification. It was clear: we had blown it.

In the boardroom, fighting for my position I was admittedly brash. The tension was suffocating. Jennifer and I stood on opposite sides, each defending our role in the task's failure. She blamed my so-called negativity and resistance to her leadership. I countered with the facts—her lack of direction, her weak leadership, her inability to execute.

Carolyn and Bill had already advised Trump to fire Jennifer. The decision should have been clear. But when we were called back into the boardroom, something shifted.

Trump wasn't looking for logic—he was looking for submission. He wanted me to beg. To plead for my spot. To ask for his mercy. I refused.

Unbeknownst to me, behind the glass, Martha Stewart watched, standing with Mark Burnett and Jay Bienstock, learning how to fire before launching *The Apprentice: Martha Stewart*. Cameras were rolling, and this was meant to be a teaching moment.

Trump went off script.

"Kristi, you're too harsh. Too cold . . ." he said, slamming his hand on the table—and then, the fateful words: "You're fired."

I met his gaze, unwavering. "You're making a huge mistake,

Mr. Trump," I said, as I stood up and walked out of the board-room. I was in complete shock but left the boardroom with my integrity intact.

What I didn't know was that while I was being held for hours post-firing, chaos erupted behind the scenes. The production team was stunned. Trump himself seemed to second-guess what had just happened.

They debated bringing Jennifer and me back to reshoot the scene—this time, with Jennifer getting fired instead. Trump was willing to do it, but ultimately, Mark Burnett decided it was too late. If word got out they had manipulated the outcome, it would be disastrous. So that was it. I was done.

I climbed into the van, still processing everything, and headed to a required dinner meeting with a therapist and my prep person, Caitlyn, who had been by my side through it all. Finally, a real meal. A steak dinner never tasted so good.

Over a short conversation with our therapist, I realized I was OK. I wasn't broken. And I damn sure wasn't done.

The next day, something happened that never made it on air.

Trump called me into his office, which he had never done with a contestant before. Cameras were rolling, but the footage never saw the light of day.

He looked at me and said, "Kristi, don't change." He reminded me that it was just a show, but I assured him it was so much more to me than "a show." And then, he gave me a piece of advice that stuck with me: "If you can learn to make quick decisions—and pull just a little bit of emotion into them— you'll always have a leg up on men in the business world." Then he said something I'll never forget. He said, "Women should be running the world. Because while logic might rule the boardroom, it's that emotional instinct—when wielded correctly—that gives women the upper hand."

Not to be ruled by emotion. But to use just enough of it to make the right call, at the right time. And with that, my time on *The Apprentice* officially ended. But my story? It was just beginning.

For the first time in my life, I felt totally free. I had no obligations, no time constraints, no baby to feed, and I could literally do whatever I wanted, on top of the bliss of being in New York and having my eyes opened to such much possibility. I was having such a powerful internal transformation. I felt like a different person, and I decided to break it off with Jason. We seemed to have such different ambitions at that point.

I spent the next few weeks in New York, living in my own apartment, still technically sequestered, without even an ID. The world was my oyster, and those weeks were like rewinding the clock and giving me a chance to have a childhood. I had never truly had one. Having a baby at sixteen meant I skipped over the reckless, carefree years most teenagers take for granted. No late nights out with friends, no road trips, no lazy Saturdays without responsibility hanging over my head. Every moment of my youth had been about survival or proving myself or making sure I was strong enough to handle what life had thrown at me. But in those few weeks, it was as if God hit the pause button on my life and whispered, "Here. This is for you." And I took it all in.

The city became my playground. The energy, the endless activities, the world-class restaurants, and Broadway shows—every experience felt like a gift. I laughed harder, breathed deeper, and allowed myself to simply *be*. And for the first time in a long time, I wasn't fighting for my place. I was just living.

One of my fondest memories from those weeks in New York was taking trapeze lessons down by the bay. I had never done anything like it before. The thought of climbing that high, of letting go, of trusting the air to catch me—it was both exhilarating and terrifying. But the second I stepped onto that platform, something inside me woke up.

The instructor called out the countdown. Three. Two. One. And then I jumped. For a moment, there was nothing but the rush of wind against my skin, the weightlessness of my body soaring through the air. I felt untethered, completely free, suspended in time. I let go of the bar and reached for the instructor's hands, and when he caught me, the feeling was electric.

Years later, I would take my daughter Catelyn back to that same spot. Watching her climb the ladder, seeing the mix of nerves and excitement on her face, I felt the moment come full circle. When she finally jumped, I saw the same thrill, the same freedom I had experienced years before. We laughed, cheered each other on, and made a memory that will stay with us forever.

Being fired from The Apprentice wasn't an ending—it was an opening. A chance to experience something I never had, to reclaim a part of myself I didn't even know was missing. Sometimes, you have to let go to truly learn to fly.

* * *

As my time in New York came to an end, I knew I was leaving with more than just memories—I was leaving with a renewed sense of self. The girl who had walked into The Apprentice boardroom, standing firm in her decision not to beg, was still inside me. But now, she carried something new. A lightness. A freedom. A realization life isn't just about proving yourself—it's about *living*. I had spent so much of my life pushing forward, carrying weight most people my age never had to bear. But in those few weeks, I had tasted something different. I had been given a glimpse of the girl I could have been, and maybe, in some ways, the woman I was always meant to become.

I wasn't just leaving New York. I was stepping into the next chapter of my life. And for the first time in a long time, I wasn't looking back over my shoulder.

CHAPTER 5

Finding the Voice I Never Lost

Shedding Criticism, Drawing from Deep Within

"Don't read the blogs." My publicist's stern warning echoed in my ears as I logged on to my computer to read the blogs. Heart pounding, curiosity bubbling—how could I resist? It was just a few weeks after my time filming *The Apprentice*. The show was now airing, and the buzz around the season was literally everywhere. It was 2005—a time before social media dominated every second of our lives. Blogs, however, started to gain traction, and they had become the go-to place for commentary and criticism.

Facebook had just launched, but it hadn't yet exploded into the cultural behemoth we know today. In some ways, I'm grateful for that. The idea of dealing with real-time criticism from every corner of the internet is overwhelming even now. But back then, blogs carried enough weight to leave scars, and I was about to find out just how deep they could cut.

I clicked through one blog after another, both eager and anxious to see what people posted. I expected some negative comments; I knew not everyone would like me. That's part of putting yourself out there. But what I didn't expect

51

was the sheer intensity of the criticism of one specific thing: my voice.

"Her accent is unbearable."

"Why can't she speak properly?"

"Another example of Southern accents and stupidity."

Each comment struck like a dagger. My Southern drawl— something I had never before thought twice about—was suddenly my Achilles' heel. It wasn't just a critique of my performance; it felt personal, like an attack on who I was at my core. By the time I shut my laptop, I was crushed.

As the days turned into weeks, the weight of those words settled over me like a heavy fog. I replayed the comments in my mind over and over, each one louder and sharper than the last. I started second-guessing every syllable I spoke and every word coming out of my mouth.

If my voice was such a problem, the solution seemed simple: stop using it.

And so, I did.

For the next sixteen years, I avoided being on video at all costs. I dodged opportunities requiring me to speak publicly, refused to record myself, and retreated into the safety of silence. The vibrant, vocal woman who appeared on *The Apprentice* faded into the background, replaced by a muted shadow. I had given my power away. I let it slip through my fingers because a few faceless strangers on the internet decided my voice wasn't good enough.

Every time I thought about speaking up, those harsh words would echo in my mind, paralyzing me. I had internalized the criticism so deeply it began to color every interaction, every relationship. I started avoiding conversations where I might be the center of attention. Social gatherings became daunting.

Even with my family, I kept things surface-level, fearing too much sharing would lead to judgment.

The silence wasn't just external; it seeped into my soul. My fear of judgment became a self-imposed prison, and my sentence lasted years.

* * *

I had an inner nagging inside about the way I was short-changing myself and my purpose. I knew I had to do something to fix it. Coming to terms with the fact I had let critics steal my voice wasn't easy. It required more than just a change in perspective—it demanded a transformation in my soul. I had to confront the reality I had let others—people I didn't even know—dictate my worth.

One pivotal moment in my journey back to confidence came when I stumbled upon a verse in the Bible that resonated deeply: "But as for you, be strong and do not give up, for your work will be rewarded" (2 Chronicles 15:7). When I read that verse, I realized God had given me my voice—literally and metaphorically. Hiding it was not only robbing me but robbing the people I was designed to reach in the world. This verse became my lifeline. It reminded me my voice, no matter how criticized, had a purpose.

I started on a journey to reclaim the voice I never lost but buried. Slowly, I began sharing my thoughts with close friends and family, testing the waters to see if I could come out of my shell and trust myself again.

I started with baby steps, recording voice notes instead of writing things down. I began forcing myself to record real estate videos—that I never published. Each small victory felt monumental. I could feel fragments of my old self returning, little by little. But the real turning point came when I decided to record a short video message for a project I was passionate about.

I set up my camera, took a deep breath, and pressed record. My heart raced as I started to speak. The initial dread was overwhelming, but I pushed through. By the time I finished, tears streamed down my face—not from sadness but from relief. I had faced a fear controlling me for far too long.

The feedback I received on that video was overwhelmingly positive. People connected with my authenticity, and for the first time in years, I felt truly seen and heard. My voice—Southern accent and all—had value. The very thing I'd become so insecure about became the bridge connecting me to others.

After that, I began creating more videos, each one chipping away at the fear and doubt keeping me silent. I started to see the power of my voice wasn't in its perfection but in its authenticity. Sharing my highs and lows didn't make me less; it made me more relatable. My voice became a tool for healing, for myself and for others who resonated with my story.

* * *

When I look back on those years, the greatest tragedy wasn't the criticism itself; it was how quickly I willingly handed my power over to someone I didn't even know. I gave a total stranger the authority to define my worth and determine whether my voice—my story—mattered. I let their words write the narrative for my life instead of writing my own.

But here's the truth: our stories matter. My story, your story. It's not just about finding your voice; it's about holding onto it with everything you have. Because your voice isn't just for you. It's for the people who need to hear it, who need to know they're not alone.

I've learned that sharing my story, in all its raw and messy glory, creates connection. It's not about perfection. It's about truth. The moments we think make us weak—the failures, the heartbreaks, the insecurities—are often the very moments making us relatable. They're the moments making us human.

> Tell your story with the kind of conviction that leaves no room for doubt.

Reclaiming my voice wasn't just about me; it was about refusing to let anyone else silence me again. And if there's one thing I want you to take away from this chapter, it's this: never let anyone take your voice away.

You will face criticism. That's a guarantee. People will question your choices, your abilities, even your worth. But their opinions don't define you. The only person who gets to decide your value is you and God. And let me tell you, He thinks you are pretty valuable.

So speak up. Tell your story. Not everyone will listen, and that's OK. The people who need to hear it will. And in sharing your truth, you'll find freedom—freedom to be fully, unapologetically yourself.

If you've ever felt the sting of criticism or the weight of someone's disapproval, know this: it can be suffocating, but it does not define you. It's natural to shrink back, to silence yourself in the face of judgment, especially when the words feel so sharp and personal. Remember this: criticism says more about the critic than it does about you. Let this truth sink in: your voice matters. It carries the power to change lives, starting with your own.

When I gave my power away to a stranger on the internet, I allowed their opinions to shape how I saw myself. They didn't know me. They didn't know my heart, my journey, or the battles I had fought to get where I was. And yet, for years, their fleeting words held more weight than the truth I knew about myself. Looking back, I see how much I lost in that silence. Opportunities slipped through my fingers. Moments to connect and make an impact passed me by because I let fear hold the microphone.

No more.

The moment I started speaking again—the moment I chose to reclaim my voice—I felt something shift inside of me. I wasn't just speaking for myself anymore. I was speaking for every person ever made to feel small. For every person who had been silenced by doubt, by fear, or by a culture that tells us we should only speak if our words are perfect and polished.

Your voice is not just about what you say—it's about who you are. It's the bridge between your experiences and the people who need to hear them. Your voice doesn't have to be perfect; it just has to be honest. When we speak from a place of truth, we create space for others to do the same.

If someone has caused you to shrink back, shut down, or play small, it's time to take your power back. Reclaiming your voice isn't just an act of self-expression; it's an act of self-love. When you speak up, you honor your experiences, your journey, and your worth. Don't hold back—share your story, even when it's scary. The world needs what only you can give.

Remember: you are not here to shrink. You are not here

to blend in. You are here to take up space, to make noise, to tell your story in a way that demands to be heard.

Because your story matters.

* * *

I want to share some practical steps that helped me find and reclaim my voice. See what resonates with you and start one step at a time. You know, getting back up is about taking things one step at a time. It's celebrating the little wins and supporting each other along the way.

Start Small: I began by recording voice notes just for myself, to hear how I really sounded. Eventually, I moved up to video recordings. Ironically, while I recorded countless videos over the years, I never shared them. Watching and listening to myself was a big step in building my confidence. Every little step forward felt like a win, and trust me, celebrating those small victories matters a lot.

Seek Support: Surround yourself with people who lift you up—this has been a game-changer for me. It's incredible how during a time when I wasn't sharing my videos more and more people started complimenting my Southern accent, which I was self-conscious about. Finding a community that values what you have to say and encourages you to speak up makes a huge difference. It helps you feel supported and valued for your unique perspective.

Embrace Vulnerability: Opening up and being vulnerable can be scary, I know. But it's also incredibly powerful. Sharing your true self allows for deeper connections with others. It's about showing up, being real, and letting people in, which turns vulnerability from a weakness into one of your greatest strengths.

Focus on Progress, Not Perfection: This was a big one for me. Let go of the idea of being perfect—it's just not realistic. Focus on making progress, no matter how small. Every time you speak up, you're stepping forward. Celebrate that because it's your journey of improvement that really counts.

Celebrate Your Uniqueness: Your voice, your accent, your tone, your style—it's all uniquely yours. Embrace these aspects of who you are instead of trying to conform to someone else's idea of perfect. The love and compliments I received for my accent when I finally started sharing my voice were a testament to this. These are what make you special and your voice worth hearing.

Practice Regularly: Just like anything else, the more you practice using your voice, the more natural it'll feel. Start with low-pressure situations and gradually work your way up. Consistency builds confidence, so keep at it, and you'll find your voice grows stronger every day.

Just start with one small step and celebrate your progress along the way. You've got this, and I'm here cheering you on every step of the way. Let's keep lifting each other up and finding our voices together. Because the only thing more powerful than one voice is our collective voices together. That's when we're unstoppable.

Through this journey, I've come to understand deeply the immense value of my voice—not just as a tool for communication but as a testament to who I am. Reclaiming it has been one of the most empowering steps I've ever taken. Every time I speak now, I do so with the firm knowledge that my voice matters. It holds value, meaning, and purpose. I've resolved never to let anyone take that away from me again.

You never know whose life you might touch with your words, whose spirit you might uplift, or whose perspective you might shift.

* * *

So here's my plea to you: let your voice be heard. Even when it shakes, even when it feels vulnerable—use it. The world doesn't need another watered-down version of someone trying to fit in; it needs the full force of who you are, exactly as you are. It doesn't need another perfect voice; it needs an authentic one. And the more you embrace yours, the more you give others permission to embrace theirs.

Somewhere out there, someone is waiting to hear it. Someone is waiting to find freedom in your words, to see themselves reflected in your journey. And if you stay silent, if you keep your story locked away, you rob them of that chance. We do not heal in silence. We do not change the world by whispering truth in the dark.

So this is your invitation.

Speak up.

Stand tall.

Tell your story with the kind of conviction that leaves no room for doubt.

Shout it to the mountaintops; let it echo through the valleys; let it carry across oceans and find the ears that need to hear it most.

Because your voice is power. Your story is freedom. And the world is waiting to hear what only you can say.

Don't let fear steal that from you.

CHAPTER 6

Behind Closed Doors

Love isn't Always Enough to Fix What's Broken

After returning home from *The Apprentice*, life picked up fast. I started buying commercial real estate in downtown Gainesville, GA. I would get a business started and make it profitable and then sell it. I built and sold quite a few small businesses: a restaurant, an apothecary store, a children's boutique, a magazine, real estate, and the last business I started was in honor of Mr. Trump—"You're Fired" Pottery Studio, which is still there today.

In the middle of all that momentum, there was something else stirring—a relationship paused for a season. Jason and I had been engaged before *The Apprentice*, but with the show filming and life moving in lightning speed, we agreed to postpone the wedding. In the whirlwind of New York City and all the "lights, camera, action," I wasn't sure what I really wanted. But after getting back to "normal," whatever that meant, my heart knew what it wanted—a life with Jason. My parents were elated and so were his, so we let them plan the wedding. Jason and I were both busy with our businesses anyway, so it worked out.

The wedding was a three-day event straight out of a fairy-tale. There was no detail overlooked, from a children's choir to a handbell orchestra. I didn't enter from the back like every-one else did. I came down from the side, through the apple orchard, which no one expected. It was magical, meaningful, and everything you'd imagine a Southern celebration would be. What I loved is that many of my childhood friends and *The Apprentice* cast had the chance to meet each other.

When Jason and I got married, it felt like the start of a dream come true. He wasn't just my husband; he was my best friend—the person I wanted to share every moment of my life with. We loved each other so deeply, so fiercely, that it felt like nothing in the world could tear us apart. Our connection was built on a foundation of trust, laughter, and shared dreams. We believed in each other in ways beyond words, and I truly thought our love could conquer anything life threw our way.

Jason adopted Catelyn shortly after we wed. It was a moment of new beginnings, a fresh start filled with hope, love, and the promise of family. But as with any journey, it was not without its difficulties, and what began with joy would even-tually unravel in ways I hadn't anticipated.

Soon after, we welcomed our second daughter, Mary Elizabeth, and her arrival was nothing short of miraculous—but not without its own set of storms.

Having a baby at age sixteen and then at twenty-five were two entirely different experiences, though both were sudden. The morning of her birth, I had just dropped Catelyn off at gymnastics where she'd be for the next few hours. She was an accomplished gymnast by then, dedicated and focused, and I knew she was in good hands. From there, I drove straight to Dr. Martin's office. Yes, the same Dr. Martin who delivered me, made sure my Catelyn had a fighting chance. As soon as I arrived, they didn't waste any time. After a quick exam, I was told to go directly to the hospital. I could feel something wasn't right; I was in excruciating pain.

I made a few quick phone calls to be sure Catelyn was picked up safely and then headed straight to labor and delivery. Dr. Martin had already called ahead and brought in reinforcements—his son who had joined his practice and was now on the way. What I didn't know was that the vertical incision from my first emergency C-section had begun to reopen on the inside. The scar tissue had become so severe my body simply couldn't hold any longer.

Born at just thirty-two weeks, Mary Elizabeth came into this world fighting, much like her sister. She faced serious complications right away. One of her lungs collapsed, requiring a chest tube, then blood transfusions followed. Monitors beeped constantly around her tiny body, and the NICU again became our world.

This time, I didn't share the news right away. The first few days were touch-and-go, and the fear of losing her was so raw and so real that we kept it to ourselves.

But just like her sister, she was a fighter. Knowing her now, I wouldn't have given life a second thought. Even in her fragility, Mary Elizabeth carried a quiet strength. I could look at her and see she was already a force to be reckoned with. I just felt it as a mother.

Once Mary Elizabeth was delivered, both Dr. Martins worked side-by-side for the next forty-five minutes carefully cauterizing and removing the layers of built-up scar tissue and stitching me up with incredible precision and care. I still remember lying there grateful beyond words not just for their skill but for the peace that fell in the midst of what could've been another traumatic delivery. They treated me like more than a patient. They treated me like someone they really truly cared about. And in those sacred moments, I realize just how much trust I had placed in their hands and, more importantly, how much God had placed the right people around me once again.

* * *

Our family of four looked idyllic from the outside. What others didn't see—what I couldn't see—was Jason struggled in ways hidden behind the facade of our happy family. His battle with addiction began after having back surgery. What started out as a way to relieve back pain became an occasional escape, a way to numb the stress of life, and slowly began to erode the foundation of our marriage. It could easily happen to anyone in the same circumstance. The stronghold of addiction is a silent enemy. We share not to shame but to shed light.

In the beginning, it was easy to dismiss. He worked long hours, the weight of fatherhood was heavy, and we were adjusting to life with two children. It seemed like the pressures of life were catching up to him, and we both chalked it up to that. But over time, I began to realize the addiction wasn't just something temporary. It wasn't just a reaction to stress. It was slowly, quietly consuming him, and with it, it was eating away at everything we had built together.

The love between us that once felt so strong now felt strained. The connection that felt so effortless now began to fray. I found myself holding on to him, trying to pull him back, trying to fix what was slipping away before my eyes. I couldn't reconcile the person I had married with the person now sitting in front of me. I couldn't understand how someone

I loved so deeply could be so lost, and I couldn't understand how to make him see the damage being done to him—to us. I wanted so badly to believe that if I loved him enough, if I was patient enough, if I just tried harder, things would get better. I wanted to believe our love was enough to heal him, that the deep connection we shared could save us both.

But what I learned, in the hardest way possible, was that love isn't always enough to fix what's broken.

> Growth doesn't happen in the easy times.

There are some battles you cannot fight for someone else.

There are some things you cannot control, no matter how much you want to.

I couldn't fix him. I couldn't make his pain go away, and I couldn't stop the spiral he was on. I couldn't stop him from hurting himself, and in my desperation to hold everything together, I started losing myself. I was drowning in the weight of trying to fix him, trying to fix us, and in the process, I was losing sight of who I was.

It wasn't just the addiction hurting us. It was the realization that, no matter how much I loved him, I wasn't enough to make it better. The girl who could reach any goal she set her mind to . . . me . . . I couldn't save our family, and it broke me. Every attempt to "fix" the situation pushed me further away from him and from the person I was meant to be. In my desperation, I lost focus of what mattered most: my own well-being, my children's well-being, and ultimately, the health of the relationship we once shared.

I wish I could say I found a way to make it work, but I came to understand that sometimes love means knowing when to let go. The hardest decision I ever made was the one to walk away, knowing I could no longer enable the cycle, knowing I had to choose myself and my children over hope. Our marriage, as beautiful as it once was, had become a toxic space I couldn't continue to live in, not without losing myself completely.

It wasn't an easy choice. Walking away from someone you love so deeply is never easy. And yet, through that heartbreak, I also learned something incredibly important about the power of resilience. Walking away didn't mean giving up. It meant recognizing I deserved better, my children deserved better, and the love we had once shared couldn't survive in a space no longer healthy for us.

In the aftermath, as I began to heal, I started to realize the love we once shared, though beautiful and deep, wasn't enough to hold us together when addiction was the silent third partner in our marriage. I began to focus on the strength I had within myself, the strength I had learned to rely on when I was a teenage mother, the strength that had carried me through so many other trials in life. And in that strength, I found my way forward.

But I also learned that love, when it's real, is not just about staying together when things are easy. Love is about knowing when to let go, when to walk away for your own good, and when to choose what's best for you and your family. Love is not about fixing someone else. It's about supporting them while they fight their own battles. But sometimes, the most loving thing you can do is let them fight those battles alone so that you can continue to fight for yourself and your future.

And now, I look back on that time, not with regret but with gratitude. Because while my marriage didn't survive, I learned some of the most valuable lessons of my life. I learned my worth doesn't come from fixing others but from knowing when to step back and take care of myself. I learned that no matter how much I loved someone, I couldn't make them better if they weren't willing to fight for themselves. And most importantly, I learned it's OK to walk away from something that is no longer serving you, no matter how deep the love is. Because sometimes, the hardest part of love is knowing when it's time to let go and trust you can rise again.

When the dust settled from the end of my marriage, I was left with more than just the weight of a broken heart. I had two beautiful children to raise, and above all else, I knew I needed to ensure they were surrounded by love, respect, and stability. Despite the pain, despite the hurt, one thing became very clear to me: it was never about us. It was about them.

Co-parenting, when done with a heart rooted in love and respect, can be one of the greatest gifts you can give to your children. Even in the midst of our most challenging seasons, Jason and I managed to find a way to put our differences aside and prioritize what was best for our kids. It wasn't easy, but I've come to understand how essential it was to give them an environment where they felt safe, loved, and supported by both parents—no matter what. And when you make it all about the kids, they feel it. They feel the peace, they feel the consistency, and they feel the security of knowing that, despite the changes around them, they are still loved and cared for by both sides.

Now that my children are young adults, I can see how deeply the co-parenting we did impacted them. They've told me time and again how much they appreciated the way Jason and I worked together to make their lives as stable as possible during that time. They saw us put our differences aside for their well-being, and they felt the strength of that love. Even though the road was rocky, the way we showed up for them created a foundation they've carried with them into adulthood. They've told me the way we handled it made them feel secure in their own relationships, that it helped them understand what real love and respect look like, even when life doesn't go according to plan.

I am incredibly proud of how we navigated the ups and downs, and honestly, I'm even more proud of how Jason and his family have remained a part of our lives. Jason's family, especially, has become so dear to me. My mother- and father-in-law are some of the most loving, grounded, "salt-of-the-Earth" kind of people you'll ever meet. They've shown me the depth of true kindness, and their love has extended far beyond what I ever expected. They've been supportive and loving toward my children, and they've been there for me in ways I will always cherish. They are, and always will be, part of my family—people I hold in the highest regard. It's a testament to the strength of love and the power of putting your heart into something that truly matters.

Co-parenting taught me so much about resilience, about the strength of love, and about how we can rise from the ashes of our past to create something better for the future. It showed me that even in the hardest times, when everything feels like it's falling apart, we have the power to choose how we show up. And when we choose to make it about the kids, when we choose love and respect, we plant seeds that will bear fruit for years to come.

While my marriage with Jason didn't last, the bond I share with his family has remained steadfast. The love they showed me through all the challenges continues to remind me that family isn't just about the blood you share—it's about the love you give and the grace you extend. And while our situation hurt us deeply, I've learned that sometimes the most painful chapters of our lives are there for a bigger purpose. Our heartbreaks, our struggles, they aren't just for us—they're for something much greater. God doesn't promise us an easy path, but He does promise that all things will work together for good, and time and time again, I've seen that truth woven throughout my life.

Romans 8:28 tells us, "And we know that in all things God works for the good of those who love Him, who have been called according to His purpose." That scripture has been a constant reminder to me that nothing we go through is wasted. Our pain, our losses, our brokenness—they are not for nothing. God can take the mess of our lives and use it to create something beautiful, something meaningful. Even when things felt hopeless, I had to trust He was using those experiences to shape me, to shape my children, and to help me reach others who needed to hear that healing is possible.

* * *

Growth doesn't happen in the easy times. There's wisdom in the struggle, growth in the pain, and beauty that emerges when we choose to keep moving forward, even when the path is unclear. And while life doesn't always make sense in the moment, it's incredible to witness how God truly does work everything together for our good.

I don't believe any of us were meant to go through life without challenges, without heartbreak. But I do believe

everything we experience can be used for a greater purpose—
whether it's to help us grow, help others, or both. And when
we walk through the tough times, keeping our eyes on what
really matters, we find healing is possible. We find our lives
can be woven together in ways far more beautiful than we
could have ever imagined. And through it all, we can trust
God is using every experience—good and bad—for our ulti-
mate good.

As time passed, one of the most profound and healing
aspects of this journey has been seeing Jason's transformation. After all the heartache, the struggles, and the painful
chapters we lived through, Jason made the decision to take
control of his life. He made a choice to be free from the chains
of addiction once consuming him. Today, he has been alcohol
and drug-free for many years, and I couldn't be prouder of the
strength he's shown.

It hasn't been an easy road for him—recovery rarely is—
but his commitment to change and to being a better version
of himself has been nothing short of inspiring. The man I
married, the one I loved so deeply, was buried under the
weight of addiction for too long. But the man he is today,
free from those destructive habits, is someone who continues to grow and evolve. Jason's recovery isn't just a personal
victory for him; it's a testament to the power of transformation, of redemption, and of the resilience lying within each
of us.

Seeing him sober and working hard to maintain that
sobriety has been a source of healing for me as well. It's
allowed us to find a sense of peace, to co-parent in a way
reflecting the positive changes we've both made. As a family, we have been able to put aside the past, not to forget it

but to learn from it and move forward in a healthier, more supportive environment for our children. It's not just about the absence of addiction—it's about the presence of healing, effort, and the willingness to be a better person for the ones we love.

Jason's sobriety has not only improved our relationship as co-parents but has also deepened our understanding of the importance of second chances. It's a beautiful reminder that no one is beyond redemption and healing is possible, no matter how broken things may seem. I believe Jason's decision to get clean and stay clean is a gift—not just for himself but for our children and for me. It has helped create an environment of respect, understanding, and healing. We no longer carry the weight of addiction; instead, we've created a space where our children can feel secure, loved, and supported by both parents.

His journey hasn't been easy, and there were times when I questioned if he could truly change. But watching him prove it to himself, to me, and to our family has been one of the most rewarding parts of this story. His sobriety is a testament to the power of choice, of resilience, and of the human spirit. And as much as I wish we could have avoided the pain we both went through, I also know this chapter of our lives—one of healing, transformation, and growth—has made all the difference in the lives of our children.

Jason's sobriety is a powerful symbol of what can happen when we choose to rise, when we choose to face our struggles head-on, and when we choose to love ourselves and each other through it all. It's a testament to the power of new beginnings, of second chances, and of the unbreakable bond that can exist in a family committed to healing.

Through all the pain, through all the brokenness, we've found something beautiful on the other side. And for that, I am endlessly grateful.

I won't pretend it was easy. Choosing to co-parent from a place of peace took effort, patience, and a willingness to put my ego aside. But looking back, I can see how every choice Jason and I made to prioritize our children over our own pain created an unshakable foundation for them.

Because at the end of the day, children don't need perfection; they need presence. They need to see love isn't just in words but in actions. That respect doesn't end when a relationship does. That family, in its truest form, isn't about who stays together—it's about who shows up, who remains consistent, who loves unconditionally.

And now, as I see my children step into their own lives, carrying with them the lessons of resilience, love, and grace, I know we did something right. They saw us fight for peace instead of against each other. They saw us honor our roles as parents, even when we couldn't honor the marriage we once had. They saw us choose love in a way that would serve them for a lifetime.

To anyone walking this path, I say this: co-parenting is not about you. It is about the children watching, learning, and forming their own understanding of what love and family truly mean. And when you choose to do it well, when you choose to co-parent with grace, you give them a gift outlasting every hardship—a legacy of love they will carry into their own families one day.

So show up. Do the work. Love your children more than you dislike your past. And above all, remember this: healing is possible. Peace is possible. A beautiful future is possible. And through co-parenting done well, your children will see love, in its purest form, always finds a way to endure.

Looking back now, I don't see failure; I see faithfulness. God was there in the unraveling, just as he was in the rebuilding. He was there in the hard conversations, the heavy goodbyes, and in the quiet victories no one else could see. And even in the seasons that broke me, he never left me empty-handed.

We don't always get to choose how our stories unfold. But we do get to choose what we do with what we've been given. I chose to heal. I chose to show up. I chose to keep walking forward.

So if you find yourself in a place where something sacred has fallen apart, take heart. Beauty can rise from broken things. It always does when God has a hand in the story.

CHAPTER 7

Looking for Love, Finding Myself

The Beautiful Ache of Surrender

As a single mom again, I continued to pour myself into real estate and business. I was focused, resilient, and doing what I had to do for my children and myself. Then, years later, I thought I had finally found love again.

It was someone I had known professionally. He started flirting one day, and suddenly, I saw him differently. The conversation felt light. Exciting. Unexpected. What began as casual became something more, and before long, we were swept up in a whirlwind romance.

Six months later, we married.

At the time, it felt like the start of something beautiful. I believed the chapter of heartache and disappointment was finally behind me. This was my fresh start—a second chance at love, a dream unfolding. We were building a blended family, navigating the complexity of bringing two lives together, and I genuinely believed everything was falling into place.

I remember thinking, *This is it. This is the story I've been waiting to write.*

But once again, it didn't take long for the cracks to show.

What appeared to be an exciting beginning quickly became a journey filled with unexpected hurdles.

Things I hadn't seen before—maybe things I didn't want to see—started to surface. Little things at first. Then bigger ones. And slowly, the picture-perfect story began to blur.

The reality of blending two families was more complicated than I'd anticipated. I had entered the marriage with hope and high expectations, but I wasn't prepared for the emotional weight that came with it—the push and pull of parenting, the tensions creeping in, the unspoken assumptions building invisible walls between us.

At first, I tried to hold it all together. I worked harder. I leaned in. I tried to be understanding, to be patient, to be the glue. But over time, the weight became too much to carry.

The separation was abrupt.

It shattered what I thought was solid ground beneath my feet.

Never in my wildest dreams did I imagine I'd be walking through divorce again. I had believed so strongly in the love we shared. I cherished that love. I thought it would be the foundation I could count on.

But love, I've learned, isn't enough—not on its own.

It takes understanding. It takes compromise. It takes two people who are willing to grow—together.

Even after the separation, I couldn't let go—not completely.

I waited two years before filing for divorce. Two years of hoping. Praying. Wondering if maybe we could still find our way back.

I believed so deeply in the love we once had. I thought, *If I just hold on a little longer . . . if I just fight a little harder . . . maybe we can fix what's broken.*

But through those two years, I learned a painful truth: one person can't carry a marriage.

It takes both people—fully committed to the hard work, the uncomfortable conversations, the growth. It takes two willing hearts. And when I finally realized I carried more than my share, I knew I had to stop trying to save something I couldn't fix alone.

Letting go wasn't easy. It never is.

But it was necessary.

And when I finally released it—truly released it—I gave God space to do the work only He could do.

Those two years were some of the darkest days I've ever walked through. But they were also holy. Honest. Stripping.

I wouldn't want to relive them, but I also wouldn't trade them—because that season shaped me. It changed how I saw love, how I saw myself, and how I saw God.

In the waiting, I was being remade.

In those dark, silent days of waiting, I had to confront something I didn't want to admit: I had been trying to control everything.

I had always prided myself on being the one who could hold it all together—the planner, the fixer, the strong one. I thought if I just did enough, worked hard enough, anticipated every outcome, I could create the life I wanted.

But the harder I tried to control everything around me, the more chaos I created within me.

I thought control would protect me from disappointment. From pain. From failure.

But what it actually did was rob me of peace.

In that season, I began to learn what surrender really meant. I had no choice but to open my hands, loosen my grip, and give everything—my fears, my heartbreak, my need for answers—to God.

And when I did, something beautiful happened.

I found freedom.

Freedom from trying to be everything to everyone. Freedom from the pressure to perform, to prove, to hold it all together.

That freedom wasn't about giving up—it was about giving over.

For the first time, I could breathe again.

It wasn't just the weight of the marriage I released. It was the weight of believing I had to be in control of my entire life.

I realized peace wasn't something I could force into place—it came only when I stopped striving.

I didn't need to have every detail mapped out. I didn't need to know what was next.

I just needed to trust that God did.

When life took that unexpected turn, I found myself standing at a familiar place: the crossroads of the unknown.

The separation had unraveled so much. I was left with a life in pieces, unsure where to begin again. But I knew I needed something different—something that would ground me in a new chapter, something that would help me rebuild not just my circumstances, but my*self*.

So I made a bold decision.

I moved.

I packed up my life and left behind the familiar, heading for the mountains and lakes of North Georgia—Rabun County. A place I barely knew. A place where I knew almost no one. A place that felt like a blank canvas.

And somehow, that unfamiliar place became the beginning of something sacred.

From the moment I arrived, something in me settled.

The mountains, the lakes, the stillness—they felt like more than scenery. They felt like an *invitation*.

At the time, I was just beginning to learn the ropes with my mentor, Lynda Hester. She poured into me—guiding me, encouraging me, helping me find my footing in a place that felt as unfamiliar as it did full of promise.

With her help, I began to grow—not just as an agent but as a woman stepping into herself again.

> This time, I wasn't chasing the picture perfect life; I was living a real one.

Then came the nudge.

Start your own firm.

I opened *Rabun Realty*—a boutique real estate firm built around a deep belief in helping people find *home* in this stunning part of the world.

Looking back now, I see it so clearly: none of this would have happened if life hadn't fallen apart first.

The career. The peace. The community. The joy.

It was all born in the ashes of a chapter I never wanted to live—but one I'm now so thankful for.

As I began to settle into life in Rabun County, something unexpected happened.

I stopped performing.

For so long, I had tried to be "superwoman." I wanted to prove I was OK, prove I could do it all, prove I had it together—even when I was barely holding on.

But here, in this new place, I allowed myself to show up differently. Not as the polished version. Not as the fixer or the fighter.

Just as me.

Imperfect. Honest. A little messy. And finally, real.

And that's when everything started to change.

My relationships deepened—both personally and professionally. The more I took off the mask, the more I was met with grace. The more I allowed myself to be *seen*, the more I discovered I wasn't alone in the struggle.

Other women began to connect with me in ways I never expected. Because when I showed up as my whole self—flawed, learning, still healing—I became relatable.

And in being real, I became *free*.

I realized what I once thought were weaknesses—my pain, my questions, my failures—were actually bridges to connection.

I had spent so long striving for perfection, but perfection never built anything meaningful.

Authenticity did.

The more I leaned into who I really was, the more peace I found. And with that peace came a deeper sense of purpose.

I wasn't just surviving anymore.

I was beginning to *live*.

Now, as I look back, I see the beauty I couldn't see in the middle of it.

The brokenness, the uncertainty, the move, the surrender—it all led me here.

I found a home. Not just a place to live, but a place to *be*. A community that welcomed me. A rhythm that finally fit. A version of myself I hadn't known before but had been waiting to meet.

And most unexpectedly, I found love again.

Not just romantic love, though that, too, came in a way

that felt like joy returned. The kind of love that makes you feel like a kid again. The kind that finds you skinny dipping off the boathouse without a care in the world.

But more than that—I found love for *my life*.

I found it in deep friendships, in meaningful work, in laughter that didn't come with a mask.

Because this time, I wasn't chasing the picture-perfect life. I was living a real one.

A surrendered one.

A life not built on control but on trust.

And just when I thought the hardest storms were behind me, life reminded me of something powerful:

Peace doesn't always mean quiet.

And strength doesn't always roar.

Sometimes it's found in stillness.

In presence.

In the silence that speaks louder than words ever could.

Because sometimes, the very moments meant to break us . . . are the ones that reveal who we really are.

If you find yourself standing where I once stood—wondering if you can start again, questioning whether you're strong enough to rebuild—I want you to know something:

You can.

You are not too far gone. It is not too late. Second chances don't have to look like the story you imagined—they can be even better than what you thought you wanted.

Maybe you're in the middle of something that feels like it's falling apart. Maybe you've let go or you're still holding on. Maybe you're walking into an unknown place with trembling hands and a quiet kind of hope.

That's OK.

Because second chances don't start with perfection. They start with surrender.

They start when you stop trying to prove you're fine and start trusting that healing takes time—and that God isn't done with your story.

I thought I needed to rebuild the life I lost. What I didn't know was God was building something new—something better.

You don't have to have it all figured out. You don't need a ten-step plan. You just need to take the next right step.

Second chances aren't always loud. They often begin in quiet places—with a whispered prayer, a brave decision, or the simple act of choosing yourself again.

So if today feels heavy, if you're tired, if you're not sure what comes next . . .

Take a breath.

Open your hands.

And know this:

There is still time.

There is still hope.

And there is a second chance waiting for you—one that may just lead you to a life more beautiful than you ever imagined.

CHAPTER 8

Follow the Trailblazers

No One Arrives on Their Own

Over the years, I've often looked at where I am and thought, *I wouldn't be here without them.* The trailblazers. The mentors. The ones who walked ahead of me and turned back just long enough to say, *"Come on. You've got this."*

They didn't just teach me—they *shaped* me.

Mentorship, I've learned, is one of the most powerful forces in shaping who we become. It's not just about knowledge. It's about wisdom. Guidance. The passing down of hard-won experience. And when someone chooses to pour into your life—to speak truth, to challenge you, to believe in you—it can change your future.

Looking back, I can trace almost every major turning point in my life to someone who chose to do exactly that.

I've been incredibly blessed to have people like that in my life—mentors who saw something in me before I saw it in myself. People who gave me both grace and grit. Who didn't just cheer me on when I was winning but stood beside me when I was lost, confused, or barely holding it together.

They weren't perfect. They didn't have all the answers. But they showed up. And they poured in.

And in doing so, they helped me become the woman I am today.

* * *

One of the most influential mentors in my life is Bob Tablak.

He was my boss when I was chosen for *The Apprentice*, but more than that, he became a steady source of encouragement, wisdom, and what I now call "strategic tough love."

Bob challenged me in ways I didn't always appreciate in the moment. He pushed me to grow, to sharpen my instincts, to refine my approach. Looking back now, I realize every piece of feedback—even the ones that stung—was a gift. A lesson. A seed that would take root in later seasons.

For more than twenty years, Bob has been more than a mentor—he's been a *constant*. Someone who always saw potential in me, even when I couldn't see it for myself.

He taught me lessons that extended far beyond business.

He showed me the importance of being approachable. That leadership isn't about flexing authority—it's about building connection. Clients, colleagues, employees . . . they need to know you're human. That you'll listen. That you *see* them.

Bob had a way of making people feel heard without ever making them feel small.

And then there was his lesson on tone.

"Kristi," he'd say, "it's not just what you say. It's how you say it."

Whether I was negotiating, giving feedback, or leading a team, Bob reminded me my delivery mattered. That tone could either open a door or shut one. And to this day, in high-pressure moments, I still hear his voice in my head, calling me to lead with intention and presence.

But perhaps the greatest gift Bob gave me was permission to dream big.

No matter how ambitious the vision, he never responded with doubt. He'd just smile and say, "Dream away."

He never clipped my wings. He encouraged me to fly.

And that simple belief—that I could—has echoed louder than any title, opportunity, or platform. It helped me grow into the kind of leader who does the same for others.

*　*　*

When I moved to Rabun County, I didn't just step into a new chapter—I stepped under the wing of someone who would change my life.

Lynda Hester wasn't just a mentor. She became family.

She didn't teach with formulas—she taught with her life.

When I entered the world of real estate, Lynda was the one who showed me the ropes. She taught me how to navigate contracts and negotiations, sure—but more importantly, she taught me what it means to lead with integrity.

To put relationships above transactions.

To serve, not sell.

To honor your word, even when no one's watching.

In a business world that often prioritizes image, Lynda modeled what it means to prioritize *impact*.

She poured into me not just as a professional, but as a person. A woman. A mother. A leader in the making.

Her mentorship went beyond coaching—it was covering.

She stood beside me through transitions, through doubts, through moments when I questioned whether I had what it takes. And with her steady voice and quiet strength, she reminded me that not only did I have what it takes—I was already becoming it.

I am the agent I am because of her.

I am the woman I am because of her.

Lynda taught me success isn't found in being impressive. It's found in being *consistent*.

In showing up with excellence, humility, and heart—every single day.

*   *   *

Mentorship didn't just shape my path—it shaped *me*.

And one of the greatest lessons it taught me was the value of being coachable.

Being coachable isn't about always getting it right. It's about being *willing*—willing to receive feedback, to lean into discomfort, and to admit you don't have all the answers.

I learned this early on as an athlete.

I'll never forget receiving the Coaches Award—not because I was the best player on the field but because I was the most willing to grow. That award meant more to me than any stat ever could. It represented heart. Hunger. Humility.

And those qualities have carried me through every season since.

Because whether you're running a business, raising a family, or chasing a dream, growth only happens when you stay open to being shaped.

Mentors hold up mirrors. They reflect our blind spots, our

patterns, our potential. The best ones won't just pat you on the back—they'll tell you the truth.

They won't just praise your strengths.

They'll speak to the parts of you that need to stretch.

And if you let them, those conversations—the hard, honest ones—can shape your character in ways success never could.

Mentorship taught me transformation doesn't happen by accident. It happens when you let someone see you, challenge you, and walk beside you as you rise.

> When we lift others, we rise together.

* * *

Somewhere along the way, the roles started to shift.

I went from being mentored . . . to becoming a mentor.

And let me tell you—there's nothing more humbling or beautiful than realizing your journey, your lessons, your story, might be the *spark* someone else needs to take the next step.

At first, I didn't feel qualified. I didn't feel like I knew enough or had it all together. But then I remembered something every one of my mentors had in common:

They didn't wait until they were perfect to pour into me.

They just showed up.

Mentorship isn't about having all the answers.

It's about being willing to walk with someone through the questions.

It's about saying, "I've been there," and meaning it.

It's about pulling someone up, not because you've mastered the mountain—but because you remember what it felt like to stand at the bottom.

As I've stepped into mentoring others, I've realized just how much I *still* learn in the process.

It's a two-way street.

Pouring into others refines me.

Teaching reminds me.

Leading keeps me learning.

It's a cycle—a sacred one.

And every time I invest in someone else's growth, I feel the echo of the mentors who invested in mine.

* * *

Not all mentors wear name tags.

Not all life-shapers come with a formal title.

Some of the most powerful mentors in my life didn't even realize they mentored me.

It was the colleague who took time to explain something instead of just doing it for me.

The friend who looked me in the eye and said the hard thing I didn't want to hear—but needed to.

The woman I watched from a distance—who led with grace and grit, never asking for recognition but quietly modeling the kind of strength I wanted to grow into.

Mentorship doesn't always look like structured meetings or official programs.

Sometimes, it shows up in everyday moments.

In conversations over coffee.

In gentle corrections.

In the way someone chooses to live with integrity, even when no one's watching.

The truth is we're all being shaped by someone.

And at the same time, we're shaping others—whether we realize it or not.

That's why it matters how we show up.

Why it matters that we stay open, honest, and generous with what we've learned.

Because someone is watching.

Someone is listening.

Someone is being mentored—just by the way we live.

* * *

If there's one thing I know for sure, it's this:

No one rises alone.

Behind every confident woman, every wise leader, every steady hand—you'll find someone who poured into her. Someone who stayed when it was hard. Someone who believed when it wasn't easy.

And the best way to honor the people who shaped us . . . is to *become* that for someone else.

Mentorship is more than instruction.

It's *invitation*.

It's saying: *There's room for you here. I see something in you. Let's grow it together.*

Whether you're seeking a mentor or stepping into that role yourself—know this: you don't have to be perfect to make an impact.

You just have to be *present*.

You just have to care.

So share your lessons. Share your story.
And don't hold back what life has taught you.
Because success doesn't shrink when we share it.
It *multiplies*.
When we lift others—we rise together.
That's the true legacy.
Not just what we achieve.
But who we helped become along the way.

CHAPTER 9

The Right to Remain Silent . . . but Loud

Wrong place. Wrong time. Right woman.

I was living my best life. I had rediscovered my voice, built a thriving real estate career, and started speaking publicly again, reigniting my passion to inspire others.

Every day, I was on the rise—stepping into my full potential and loving the journey. I found my place in the world, and I finally started to feel the peace I had worked so hard to create. Life felt like it was unfolding exactly the way I had dreamed. Rabun County became my sanctuary—a place where I rooted myself deeply in my career and in my heart. Here's why: Rabun County is a world that feels untouched, where nature whispers ancient secrets and every corner seems to hold a story. Nestled in the embrace of the timeless Appalachian Mountains and serene lakes reflecting the vast sky, there's a peace here that wraps around you, like a familiar, comforting blanket, softening the edges of the world and inviting you to listen to the quiet whispers of your own soul. Every evening, as the sun dips behind the soft curves of the mountains, it's as though the entire county takes a collective breath, settling into a slower, gentler pace. The cool mountain air tightens the embrace of the land, pulling shadows over the hills as the stars start to peek through.

It's in these moments Rabun County reveals its soul and leaves you breathless.

As night falls, the air fills with the rhythmic hum of cicadas—the earth itself is singing its own lullaby.

Fireflies make their entrance,

flickering like tiny stars in a slow, elegant dance

beneath the canopy of trees.

It's a sight you can't help but get lost in, their glow lighting up the quiet, shadowy woods around me. The very pulse of this land beating in perfect rhythm.

I've spent countless evenings on the porch of my renovated farmhouse, wrapped in a quilt and rocking gently to the rhythm of life all around. An old swing, on an old porch, taught me the art of stillness. In these moments, surrounded by the timeless hills that have witnessed generations come and go, I've found a place to reconnect with myself. A place to breathe deeply, to let go, and to just be. Seven years of sunrises and sunsets, each one painting a new masterpiece, leaving its mark on my life in ways I could never have imagined.

On one of those perfect June evenings, as the sun dipped behind the mountains and the fireflies began their nocturnal ballet, I sank into the familiar comfort of my home. The hours seemed to melt away as I lost myself in a book.

Feeling at peace, I slid into the calming embrace of my sheets. The air outside was fresh and cool, drifting in through the slightly open window. It was around 10:00 p.m. when suddenly there was a loud, insistent knocking on the front door. *What the hell . . .?* I jumped out of bed, heart pounding, to see flashing lights outside my window. Still in my bedclothes, I opened the front door to see two young police officers standing there.

"Kristi Caudell, I have a warrant for your arrest," one officer said.

"*Excuse me*, for what?"

"We can talk about that later; you must come with us."

He pulled out the handcuffs sending shivers up my spine.

"Well hold on a minute—"

"Kristi Caudell, you have the right to remain silent . . ."

"HOLD ON!"

My quick-thinking daughter had called the local judge, a friend of ours. She handed me the phone on speaker as we tried to sort out what the issue was. But even his voice of reason couldn't sway the officers who stood in my doorway, waving their warrant like a winning lottery ticket.

The judge finally said to me, "Kristi, you'll have to go with them for now, but we will get it all cleared up." There I stood, dumbfounded, frustrated, barely awake, and barely dressed. I turned to the officers. "Hold on a minute and let me go get some clothes on." As I turned to go to my room and at least "clothe myself in dignity," the younger officer lunged at me aggressively, snapping handcuffs on me without a word.

I was escorted out—shoeless at first, rightless entirely—and shoved into the backseat of a police car. We then sped away with zeal fit for a high-speed chase.

This is crazy! I thought.

I'm not a criminal.

I'm a mother.

I'm a barefoot, braless realtor in pajamas.

The sting of the handcuffs, the blue lights strobing against my tear-streaked cheeks—it was all profoundly humiliating.

There was nothing I could do.

I just sat there, helpless, as the tears fell—silent and steady.

Arriving at the jail felt like stepping into a spotlight of shame—exposed, vulnerable, and utterly terrified.

Powerless and voiceless, again.

I was fingerprinted and booked.

I could already feel the bruises forming from the rough handling of the officers. While I waited to bail me out, my mind was in overdrive—racing through every detail leading up to this moment. Every call, every conversation, every step replayed in a desperate loop, trying to make sense of how I ended up here.

You see, my role as a realtor has always gone beyond just buying and selling property. More often than not, I find myself standing in the middle—translating the dreams of out-of-town clients and the boots-on-the-ground reality of local contractors.

In this case, I had the pleasure of securing a stunning piece of land for a client—a place nestled among tall, exquisite pines, where they envisioned building something truly special. Acting on their behalf, I met a local grader onsite to walk potential home sites. We mapped it out thoughtfully, guided by the lay of the land and soil tests that helped us align their vision with the environment.

Later that day, just before heading to lunch with a dear friend at Ally's old store in Lakemont, I texted the grader to request a written quote. While I often sealed things with a handshake, my clients had been burned before. They insisted on something formal. The grader responded quickly, and I passed the quote along to my clients. I assumed they'd follow up from there.

Weeks passed, life got busy, and I never heard back. I mentally set the project aside.

Then the grader contacted me, insisting I come inspect the work he'd completed. Caught up in other projects, I didn't go—especially since I'd already handed things back over to the clients. I explained I was no longer involved. That's when his tone shifted.

He moved straight to payment. I reassured him my clients were good people. But then he mentioned a "contract"—one that didn't exist. That's when the pit in my stomach formed.

> Bitterness only chains us to the pain. So I chose love.

My clients had never signed anything. They never authorized the work.

The grader had moved forward without formal approval, and now that he realized he had no binding agreement with them, he came after me. Demanding I pay him out of my own pocket.

I refused. Firmly.

It wasn't my work. It wasn't my responsibility.

He became furious, throwing around threats of legal action. At one point, he even said he'd have me arrested.

I brushed it off, but did my due diligence and confirmed with my trusted friend, a judge. He was calm and clear: "There will be no arrest." And with that, I exhaled. I had no authority to commission the work, and everyone involved should have known that.

But that didn't stop what came next.

A young officer—perhaps inexperienced, perhaps over-zealous—took the grader's word as gospel. There was no investigation. No phone call. No attempt to hear my side. Just an accusation followed by handcuffs.

Forty minutes later, my attorney arrived and posted bail. I was shaken but grateful. Still, the ordeal wasn't over. Now, I wasn't just fighting for my name—I was facing a criminal trial.

* * *

Of course, word spread like wildfire in our small town, and my attorney warned me not to say a word about the matter to anyone until the trial—which would be about a year out. That summer after the arrest, Rabun County felt different. I wrestled with a strange new reality; my usual bustling routine as a realtor was now interspersed with hushed phone calls and quiet meetings with my attorney. I retreated from the public eye, my confidence shaken, my integrity questioned. Social media, once my marketplace, was now a battlefield filled with landmines. My mugshot was shared around without a second thought of how it would impact me, creating a distorted reflection of who I really was. I wasn't ready for the familiar scrutiny and disapproval of the public eye.

During those days, I retreated to Rabun County's vast natural beauty for solace. I would wander through the familiar trails and spend days on the water where I could breathe in mountain air instead of judgment.

The weeks crawled by, and the battle in my head raged with the awareness of the whispers all around me. I'm so thankful for my real friends and allies who stood by me and wouldn't let the rumors write my story. They didn't need me to speak or defend myself; they knew me, the real me, and that was enough.

One friend, a retired schoolteacher with a spine of steel, encouraged me, "Child, when they go low, we go high. We're standing with you." And stand they did.

Business mentors, those titans of the trade I had admired from afar, reached out with advice that sounded more like the epitome of bittersweet cliché. "You're really something when folks start kicking up dirt to tarnish your shine," they would say. It both soothed and burned. It meant I had truly made an impression on Rabun County but not in the way I had ever intended or desired.

In the stretched-out weeks before trial, I wanted nothing more than to speak—to shout my innocence from every rooftop in Rabun County. But I stayed quiet, heeding my attorney's counsel. Instead, I kept retreating into nature and let it minister to my soul.

One afternoon, as I left the lake, a sudden storm rolled in. The skies turned from soft blue to violent gray. With the top down on my Jeep and nowhere to pull off the narrow mountain road, I had no choice but to keep going—soaked, exposed, and wildly unprepared.

Suddenly, I realized I wasn't just in a storm—I was in a metaphor. A microcosm of everything I'd been carrying inside.

This wasn't just about the storm I was driving in; this was about the storm I was living in. And the only way out . . . was straight through.

The rain hit hard and fast. My clothes clung to my skin, my hair dripping, my hands gripping the wheel as water poured in. But strangely, it wasn't misery—it was release. The surrender to nature's wildness, to the reality of having no control, was exactly what I needed.

When I finally pulled into my driveway, the rain stopped

as quickly as it had started. The clouds parted, and golden light spilled across the glistening earth. The scent of rain-soaked pines filled the air—deep, earthy, and unforgettable. It grounded me.

That moment reminded me: God is still in control. Of the weather. Of my life. Of the outcome.

The mountain air clung to me long after that drive. It became a symbol of transformation—proof that storms pass, and what remains is stronger because of it.

As the trial date crept closer, something inside me shifted. I started to embrace silence—not as absence but as presence. The silence was full, almost musical, like it had its own language. For the first time, I realized being heard doesn't always require speaking.

Sometimes the most powerful message isn't shouted—
It's carried.
Carried with grace. Carried with dignity.

In a world full of noise, speculation, and assumptions, I chose not to explain myself.

I chose to hold my head high,
    to hold my peace,
    to hold my ground.
I chose my right to remain—
    Silent.

* * *

The morning of the trial, a heavy silence hung over me as thick as morning fog in the valleys of Rabun County. My heart was cloaked in layers of uncertainty and anxiety. Walking into the courtroom, there was an air of somber formality;

the hushed whispers of the gallery feeling like a distant hum against the drumming of my own pulse in my ears. I was about to stand before the very judge who had signed off on my warrant, and that irony was not lost on me. As I took my seat, gripping the cool surface of the defense table for grounding, my attorney, a steadfast presence beside me, was the picture of meticulous preparation. His confidence reassured, yet the fluttering in my stomach refused to settle.

The officer who had wrongfully accused me, whose grip had left its mark on my arm and on my life, cast a long shadow over the room. Yet, as the trial started and it became his turn to take the stand, his sure footing seemed to falter.

But when it came time for him to take the stand, something shifted. The certainty he once held began to crack. Under oath, under the weight of the law—and under the watchful eyes of the judge and gallery—he visibly shrunk. Sweat beaded on his forehead. He couldn't meet my gaze.

When cross-examined, his facts crumbled like dry leaves underfoot. He admitted—haltingly—he didn't know the difference between a quote and an agreement. That he had secured a warrant based on hearsay. That he hadn't reviewed the deed, hadn't done even the simplest due diligence, and hadn't bothered to hear my side.

This wasn't justice. This was laziness in uniform. A house of cards, caught in the gust of courtroom truth.

And there I sat.

Silent but loud.

My story echoed in the hollow spaces his words couldn't fill. My innocence didn't need a defense—it stood strong on its own, amplified by the silence his testimony couldn't escape.

The courtroom felt both vast and suffocating, time

stretching with each second . . . until the judge finally, mercifully, declared me acquitted.

Justice was served that day. The officer who arrested me no longer wore the badge he misused. And as I stepped out of that courthouse and into the light of day, I knew—

my silence had spoken.

And it was heard.

I had walked through fire, betrayal, and humiliation.

I wasn't just free.

I was *refined*.

* * *

Even in the silence, I heard the voice in my soul:

Girl, get up.

And I did.

Getting up wasn't just about reclaiming my name.

It was about reclaiming *me*.

I could have chosen bitterness. I had every reason to. But I knew: Bitterness only chains us to the pain. So I chose love. Not the easy kind. The bold kind.

The kind that forgives, releases, and refuses to become what hurt it.

Sometimes the hardest moments—the ones that strip us bare—are the very ones that rebuild us. It's not in the absence of pain that we grow but in the courage to face it head-on. When we stop running from the discomfort and instead choose to learn from it, we don't just survive— we transform.

Each time we rise after the fall, we become more resilient. More compassionate. More ourselves.

If you're in the middle of your own storm, hear me: this isn't the end of your story. You are being shaped, not shattered. Embrace each challenge as an invitation to rise—because true strength is found not in never falling, but in how we choose to get up and move forward after the fall.

CHAPTER 10

Love Anyway

The Bold Way Forward

Love.

One of the most used—and most misunderstood—words on the planet.

We love our *friends.*

We love our *pets*, our *partners*, our *kids.*

We also love *movies, music,* and *pizza.*

Hardly the same.

Even the way we love people changes depending on the relationship.

So let's talk about *real* love.

Not the kind that's easy, not the kind that shows up when everything is going great, but the kind that chooses to stay, to forgive, and to keep going even when it's hard.

Life has a way of knocking the wind out of us sometimes. People hurt us. We disappoint ourselves. We carry regrets, failures, and moments we wish we could undo. But here's what I've learned—love is the only way through.

Love is more than a feeling—it's an action. It's showing up, even when it's inconvenient. It's choosing grace when someone doesn't deserve it. It's speaking life into people when they've forgotten their own worth. And the most powerful thing? Love multiplies. When you pour it out, it comes back to you in ways you never expected.

Real, deep, life-giving love isn't just something we fall into; it's something we choose. Every single day.

* * *

Choosing love doesn't mean forgetting the pain. It doesn't mean pretending the wounds aren't there. It means deciding those wounds will not define my future.

Choosing love means choosing to forgive—not just others but yourself.

It means not letting your past mistakes—or someone else's—define the rest of your story.

I don't know what you're carrying right now, but if it's heavy, I want you to hear this:

You don't have to hold it forever.

You can put it down.

You can forgive.

Not because they deserve it, but because *you* deserve peace.

Forgiveness was the hardest lesson I ever had to learn.

It took wrestling with my own pride, my own pain, and my own sense of justice.

But in the end, I realized forgiveness was never about them.

It was about setting myself free.

The hardest person to forgive?

Myself.

I've held onto pain longer than I should have. I've replayed words I wish I could erase. But the moment I chose love over resentment, forgiveness over bitterness—I found freedom. And I want that for you too.

If you choose to carry bitterness, it is you who suffers the most. It poisons your soul. It keeps you trapped in the past. And I refuse to live that way.

Love is not weakness.

It is the strongest, most resilient force there is. It takes strength to let go of resentment.

It takes courage to look at the people who hurt you and say: "You will not have power over me anymore." That is what true freedom looks like.

* * *

And love isn't just for others. It's for yourself too.

Loving yourself means letting go of what no longer serves you. It means setting boundaries. It means having the courage to walk away from toxic situations and demand more for your life.

Love has been my greatest act of rebellion against every hardship that tried to break me. I have walked through hell and come out the other side with a heart that still beats with hope, with faith, with love. Not because life has been easy—but because I made a choice. A choice to love, to forgive, to rise.

* * *

I'm 5'2", blonde, blue-eyed. I don't exactly scream *powerful presence*. But I've learned: true power has nothing to do with volume. For those of us who don't fit the mold—who may be underestimated at first glance—life teaches us it's not about what people see on the surface. It's about what lives inside.

It's not about how loud you are. It's about how you show up—with love, with grace, with a presence that makes people feel safe, seen, and valued.

True leadership isn't about commanding authority. It's about earning trust. It's about seeing beyond someone's past and calling out the good in them. It's about forgiveness—not just for others, but for yourself—because holding on to resentment only weighs you down.

Love isn't loud. It's in the quiet moments.

It's the kind word.

The listening ear.

The moment of patience.

These are the things that change lives.

Whether in motherhood or business, I've seen how love changes everything.

When I look at my daughters, I don't just see them as my children—I see them as the incredible individuals they are. And the more I choose to love them as they are—not who I think they should be—the more they flourish.

Love, without conditions, gives people the freedom to step fully into who they were meant to be.

In real estate, it's the same. When I slow down to truly listen to a client's story, their fears, their dreams—something shifts. It becomes more than a transaction. It becomes a connection.

Love is the soil where people flourish.

* * *

Choosing love means choosing empathy.

It's not just imagining someone else's life. It's walking

alongside them. It's celebrating their victories like they're your own. It's carrying their pain, not because you have to—but because you care.

It's a gift, yes. But it's also a responsibility.

And while love may feel heavy at times, I wouldn't trade it for anything. Because in walking with others, in feeling deeply, we find the depth of connection we were made for.

Let's not wait for the big moments to show love. Let's make the small ones count. People may forget what you said, but they will never forget how you made them feel.

> In walking with others, in feeling deeply, we find the connection we were made for.

This chapter is deeply personal to me because choosing love has changed everything in my life. I've had to learn—sometimes the hard way—that love isn't just an emotion. It's an action. It's the conscious decision to rise again, to keep our hearts open when it would be easier to shut down, and to love even when the world tells us not to. True strength isn't found in never falling. It's found in how we choose to rise and love ourselves and others, even when it's hard.

And here's the best part—making a real impact doesn't require grand gestures. It's in the small, everyday choices. The quiet acts of kindness. The intentional conversations. The moments when you simply let someone know, *I see you. You matter.*

I've seen this in my real estate business. It's easy to rush through transactions, to keep things moving with-out slowing down. But when I take the time to truly listen to my clients, to understand their fears, their dreams, their hesitations—something shifts. Trust begins to build. And suddenly, it's not just a business deal anymore. It's a relationship. It's a connection beyond a contract.

Empathy has been one of the greatest gifts in my life. It has made my relationships richer, my work more fulfilling, and my heart more open. Yes, there have been times when it's felt heavy. When I've carried burdens that weren't mine, when I've felt exhausted from caring so deeply. But I wouldn't trade it for anything. Because when we love people fully—when we truly walk with them through their highs and lows—we find the depth of connection we were made for.

And if I've learned one thing, it's this: the greatest impact we will ever have doesn't come from the grand moments. It comes from the small, consistent choices to love—when it's inconvenient, when it's uncomfortable, when it's undeserved. A kind word. A listening ear. A moment of patience. These are the things that change lives.

I've made the decision to live with an open heart, to engage with people in a way that refuses to judge, to choose love even when it's not the easy path. And the more I do this, the more I see love ripple out—building a world that is softer, kinder, and more compassionate.

In the fall of 2024, as I walked my mother through her final season of life, this truth became more real than ever. I saw firsthand the little things—things we often overlook—are actually the big things. Holding her hand, playing her favorite music, sitting beside her in silence when there were no words left—those were the moments that mattered. The love in those small, quiet moments was everything.

People won't always remember what you did, but they will never forget how you made them feel.

So, my dear friend, I want to invite you into this journey with me. Let's choose to see people for who they really are, not for the labels they wear. Let's choose to show up with love, to extend grace, to give without expecting something in return. Because when we do, we don't just change the lives of others—we change our own.

It's not about waiting for the big moments. It's about making the small ones count.

And sometimes, it's those small, love-soaked moments that carry us through the hardest seasons, the ones where words fall short, and silence feels heavy. That's when love matters most.

So choose it. Choose love. Choose joy. Choose to walk forward with a heart that is light, with a spirit that is unshaken, and with a confidence that says, *I will not be defined by what I have been through—I will be defined by how I rise.*

Remember, love doesn't just shape how we show up for others. It prepares us for the moments when love is all we have left to hold on to love, and its truest form is what carries us through the darkest valleys, and there is no valley deeper than grief.

The kind of grief that rearranges your world, the kind that brings you to your knees, the kind forcing you to decide whether you stay down or will you rise again?

I want to take you with me into one of the darkest seasons of my life, the season of saying goodbye. Of losing people I love. Of learning to carry grief and gratitude in the same breath. It wasn't easy, but it was sacred, and it changed me forever.

CHAPTER 11

Lingering Goodbyes

Sifting Through What's Left After Loss

Grief is a deeply personal journey.

It looks different for everyone.

No two people experience loss the same way.

There's no one-size-fits-all template for navigating the storms of sorrow, and often, it can feel like a journey you have to walk alone. But what I've come to understand through the recent loss of my best friend, Lindsay, who was more like a sister and my sweet momma is that, while grief is unique, it also teaches us the universal truth that we have to choose to get up, even in our grief. We have to choose to rise, even when it feels like we can't possibly go on.

Grief has a way of knocking us to our knees, but it also has the power to reveal the deepest parts of our hearts. It challenges us to grow in ways we never thought possible. And as we find our way through it, we learn that while we may never get over our losses, we can still find ways to move forward, to live with purpose, and to honor the lives of those we've lost.

Let me take you back to March 12, 2009. My daddy had just celebrated his sixty-second birthday on January 14. That night he sat down with his birthday cake and glass of milk in hand, and with a peaceful sigh, he said, "Well at least I have ten good years left."

I remember quickly correcting him. "Oh no, Daddy, don't say that. You have at least thirty years left." I couldn't imagine losing my father in ten years, much less two years later.

What I didn't know in that moment was my daddy had already been given the gift of healing. Just days before, he stood up in church at Free Chapel, and our Pastor, Jensen Franklin, asked anyone who felt completely healed after we had completed our church-wide community fast to rise. My daddy stood, and he wasn't just standing in faith. He stood because he had truly been healed. He was healed, spiritually, emotionally, and mentally. He was a new man. Every demon that ever tried to take him out was defeated.

A couple of days later, Daddy was snoring so loudly that my mom left to run errands, not wanting to disturb his deep sleep. But a few moments after she drove away from the house, he called her on the phone and simply said, "Deb, come quick!"

She turned the car around only five minutes away. She drove home and found my dad on the porch collapsed, front door open, the phone beside him, and 911 plugged in but not sent. Mom ran over to him and started CPR. She felt a presence behind her so strongly she didn't dare turn around and look. She knew it was Daddy, and she was too late.

The autopsy confirmed it was a massive heart attack.

He was gone before his body fell to the ground.

I dreaded telling my girls. He was their pop-pop. Their hero.

I drove to Catelyn's school to tell her in person. She's an old soul, and she processes things beyond her years. When I told her, I asked if she wanted to go to the hospital and see him one last time. She did.

When we were in the hospital room, she stood beside his hospital bed, observing him quietly, then she looked up at me and said, "That's not Pop-Pop. He's really not here anymore. He's gone to be with God."

And then there was Mary Elizabeth. She was younger, still full of innocence and wonder. I told the family not to say anything to her. I wanted to tell her, and I wanted it to be when I could sit with her and help her process, not when I was planning funeral arrangements.

I came home a day later from staying at Mom's, and Mary Elizabeth ran up to me and said, "Mommy, Mommy! Pop is not with us anymore."

I looked at Jason with disapproval. How could he do this to me! Stunned, he shrugged and threw his hands up. As if to say he had not told her.

"How do you know that?" I asked her.

"Pop-Pop came to see me," she said.

"Where did Pop-Pop come to see you?" I asked.

"In your bathroom," she said. "He told me he had gone to be with Jesus."

"Really? What did he look like?"

She proudly bumped her chest and said, "He looked like me." Which means he had his blonde hair back.

Pop-Pop visited her two more times after that. The final time was in her playroom. He told her he wouldn't be back to visit again until Jesus returned.

I wish I could say I taught her about Jesus coming back, and that there was a logical explanation for everything she said she saw. But that's not the case. At that age, I hadn't even introduced that concept yet. God took care of that conversation for me. I never had to break the news to her. She was joyful for Pop and knew she would see him again. That's the kind of God we serve.

Grace is a journey that will break your heart wide open, but it will also allow you to witness miracles in the most unexpected ways.

And in those moments, we get to decide what we do next. We can stay in the pain, or we can choose to rise.

* * *

Let me tell you about my dear friend Lindsay. She was, without question, the strongest person I've ever met. From the moment I met her, I knew there was something extraordinary about her. She had been battling cancer fourteen years, and I had the privilege of walking alongside her throughout that time. What I learned from Lindsay was profound: I learned how precious life truly is, that each day is a gift. She taught me we can laugh through the hard times, joy can coexist with pain, and the human spirit is capable of extraordinary strength in the face of adversity.

Lindsay's resilience was unmatched. She never let cancer define her. Instead, she lived her life with a vibrant, contagious energy. She had a way of making even the most difficult moments feel like an adventure. I have never laughed with anyone as hard as I did with her. Our travels were always full of fun and laughter—whether we rushed back and forth to the Mayo Clinic or took spontaneous trips to Seaside, Florida, which she loved with all her heart. We explored, we relaxed, and we made memories in the way only the most carefree of friends could. However, our most favorite place was "the lake"; Lake Rabun is where we met and where Lindsay was in her full element. The lake was her happy place. A place she could heal and be in nature.

One of my most precious memories with Lindsay was spent on Lake Rabun. Those were the days we spent cruising around the lake with our friends, watching for eagles, cocktails in hand, and no agenda other than enjoying the beauty of the moment. Each day was a spontaneous adventure. No schedule, no expectations—just pure, unfiltered fun.

> Loosing those I loved deeply, forced me to confront parts of my own story that I had tucked away.

Lindsay had introduced me to some of the most wonderful people, and I consider myself so lucky and blessed to be friends with them. Every time they came around, life felt brighter and more beautiful. There was something special about the way we all came together, creating laughter and joy in the simplest of moments.

But one memory, in particular, stands out as a symbol of our friendship and the power of living fully, even in the face of illness. It was the last weekend Lindsay and I ever spent together at the lake. The rain fell gently, and we sat on the screened-in porch, looking out over the lake. It was one of those afternoons where the rain brought a quiet peace, and Lindsay turned to me with that mischievous grin of hers and said, "Let's go skinny-dipping."

Now, here's the thing: I live here. I work here. I show real estate here. But in that moment, all of that was irrelevant.

There was something in the air, something in her voice that made me drop all of my inhibitions. I didn't hesitate. I grabbed the towels, and we undressed on the porch, wrapping ourselves up and heading toward the lake.

There was a boathouse with a jumping platform, where we could swim near the cove, and then there was the open dock—a place that felt so free, so wide open. Lindsay headed to the cove for a bit more privacy, but I had other plans. I looked at her and said, "If we're going to do this, we're going to do it right." I wanted us to go to the open dock, the one that felt more daring, more "us." So we did.

It had been raining, so the lake was completely empty of boats. As we made our way to the water, the rain began to subside, and a soft, beautiful fog started to lift off the lake. We swam, and as we floated in the water, we talked. She shared her concerns about her upcoming visit to the Mayo Clinic. There was always that underlying stress, but in that moment, we didn't focus on the fear. Instead, I offered her words of encouragement, reminding her of how many times God had shown up in her life. We spoke about faith, about strength, and about the power of perseverance.

Then, something extraordinary happened. As I spoke, Lindsay's eyes widened in awe, and she pointed to the sky. A massive eagle, wings spread wide, appeared right above us, soaring low over the water. It hovered for a moment, its wings cutting through the fog as if it reached down to grab a snack from the lake, only to stop just short and ascend back into the sky. It was breathtaking—this eagle, so close, so majestic, and so powerful, soaring above us in a moment of absolute serenity. It felt as if the heavens themselves had opened up just for us.

Lindsay and I sat there, hand in hand, in complete awe. We had both been overwhelmed with emotion, and in that moment, we cried. It wasn't just the beauty of the eagle or the peacefulness of the moment—it was a reminder. A reminder God is in control, that even in the midst of illness and uncertainty, there is beauty, grace, and peace to be found. The rain had stopped, the fog had lifted, and the world felt lighter. We shared that moment together, and in it, we found a peace we both so desperately needed.

But, like all things in life, our time together on the lake came to an end. Lindsay's battle with cancer was one she fought with everything she had, but in the end, she lost the fight. I was left with an emptiness I didn't know how to fill. The pain of losing her was unlike anything I had ever experienced. We were supposed to have more adventures, more laughter, more moments together. And yet, there I was, learning how to live without her.

What I didn't know then, what I had to learn after the fact, was how Lindsay's passing would impact me in a way that went beyond grief. She passed away on my birthday. At first, that was a hard one to swallow. I remember feeling like I couldn't breathe when I realized the date, thinking it was somehow unfair, that the day meant something so different now. It felt like a loss that would never be able to heal. But as time has gone on, I've come to find peace in the fact Lindsay's heavenly birthday is the same as mine. In some ways, I feel like she's always with me now, on that special day. I cherish the fact that we shared the same birthday. Now, I'm so thankful for it. It's a reminder she's still here, in my heart, and I carry her spirit with me every single day. Our bond, our memories, and our shared laughter will forever be a part of me.

Lindsay's legacy lives on in the lessons she taught me: that life is precious, that every day is a gift, and that we have the power to create moments of beauty and joy, even in the midst of hardship. Her spirit will always be with me, in every laugh, in every adventure, and in every quiet moment of reflection by the lake.

* * *

I still processed the shock of losing her when another, even more unexpected, blow came: my mother was diagnosed with terminal cancer. It felt like the universe was testing me, throwing loss and grief in my path one after another. And yet, through it all, I have learned that while grief is a journey we never truly get over, it is also a path of growth. We don't have to let grief define us. Instead, we can use it to redefine ourselves.

My relationship with my mother was not always easy, but it was one of the most powerful relationships in my life. I spent much of my childhood and young adult years closer to my dad. I was a daddy's girl through and through. But as I grew older, especially as I navigated the challenges of adulthood, my relationship with my mom deepened in a way I never could have expected. She became one of my closest friends, someone I could turn to for advice, for comfort, and for understanding. We were able to connect in ways I never thought possible when I was younger, and those moments became some of the most cherished of my life.

But just as I had started to truly understand and appreciate her, I was faced with the gut-wrenching reality she didn't have much time left. When my mother was diagnosed, I had no idea how quickly things would change. Her health rapidly declined, and I found myself faced with the reality I would soon have to say goodbye. Even with that knowledge, nothing could prepare me for the pain of losing her. It came quickly, unexpectedly, and left a hole in my heart that seemed impossible to fill.

Despite everything, my mom's passing was beautiful and peaceful. There was no struggle. There was no pain. It was as though she knew it was time to let go, and when the moment came, she did so with grace. In a way, it was a blessing to see her go without suffering. But as much as I was grateful for the way she passed, I still felt the profound sting of loss.

I thought I had more time with her—
more moments to make new memories.
But in the blink of an eye,
that time was gone.

The hardest part of losing my mom was not the grief but the suddenness of it. Just ten days before her passing, we celebrated her life. She had always said she wanted a "celebration of life" instead of a funeral. She wanted her living to be celebrated, not her death. So we did just that.

I arranged for her favorite restaurant, Señor Fiesta in Gainesville, Georgia, to cater her celebration. Her favorite bartender, Luis, mixed up her favorite Texas margaritas—both frozen and on the rocks. The evening ended with fireworks, and it was absolutely incredible. The atmosphere was filled with joy, love, and laughter, and my mom was so full of life that night. She looked and felt so well, and as I stood there, surrounded by friends and family, I couldn't help but feel like we had so much more time together.

But in the following, everything changed.

Just ten days after that night of celebration, my mom passed away unexpectedly.

I thought I would have months—maybe even a year—to continue to care for her, to cherish her presence. But God had different plans. It was the hardest thing I had ever experienced.

Losing her was like losing the final piece of the puzzle holding my world together.

I didn't grow really close to my mom until later in life, but what I came to realize is everything I am today is shaped by both my parents—by their love, their sacrifices, and by the lessons they taught me.

I think about my mom often and how much she taught me, especially in her final years. One of the biggest lessons I learned from her was it's really the small things in life that matter the most.

It's the kind words you offer to a stranger.

It's the phone call to check in on a friend.

It's simply showing up.

These are the things that make a difference.

My mom's kindness, her genuine care for others, and her ability to find joy in the simple moments is something I carry with me every day.

Just two weeks before my mother passed, she, my daughter, and son-in-law came to spend the weekend to celebrate Catelyn and my mom's birthdays.

It would be the last time we would all celebrate together.

We didn't know it at the time.

We had a peaceful, easy weekend, relaxing, watching football, and eating really well. That Sunday morning as everyone packed up the car to head home, Mom and I found ourselves alone in the living room. We had Free Chapel on TV, and as the worship music faded and the sermon was about to begin, something shifted in the atmosphere.

She looked at me with eyes I had never seen before.

They were full of peace, clarity, and love, stopping me in my tracks.

Without a word, she gently moved the ottoman from her chair and patted the space in front of her. "Come here, baby" she said softly. I sat down on the ottoman. She wrapped me in her arms, holding me tightly, and began to gently pat my back like she would've done when I was a child. Then she cupped my face in her hands, looking directly into my eyes, and said, "I am so proud of you, and I love you so much."

The way she looked at me in that moment is something I will never forget.

Her face was radiant, almost glowing. There was a peace about her that felt heavenly. And while I couldn't find the words for it then, I knew what she was telling me without saying it outright.

She was ready.

She was at peace.

She was prepared to meet her Maker and to be fully healed.

That moment with her was a gift a holy exchange between mother and daughter that spoke volumes without needing many words. When I think of my mom, now I think of her face in that moment.

Shining.

Calm.

Full of love.

It was the most beautiful I had ever seen her.

In the months that followed, I found myself reflecting on our relationship, on everything I had learned from her, and how much of her had become a part of me. Losing her left a hole in my heart, but it also made me realize how much she had taught me. She had always been my rock, my safe place. And in the quiet moments after her death, I understood it wasn't the grand gestures that made her so special but the small things—the little acts of kindness, the quiet presence, the way she showed up for me, even when things were tough.

When I read the letter at her celebration of life service, I was overcome with emotion. I had written it from my heart, capturing the essence of who my mom was and the incredible impact she had on my life. The words I shared with everyone that day were just a glimpse into the woman she had been and the legacy she left behind.

Here's a part of what I read that day:

Today, we gather not in mourning, but in celebration—celebration of my mom's life, her strength, her love, and the deep impact she has made on each of us. As many of you know, my mom doesn't want a service after she passes, so today, we honor her while she's still with us. And if there is one word that captures her spirit, it's endure.

Watching her go from running circles around me to now spending most of her days being still has reminded me of how precious and fleeting time truly is. We don't know what tomorrow holds, and her journey has made me realize how important it is to live each day as if it were our last—not out of fear but with love, joy, and purpose.

My mom has shown me what it means to endure—not just in the sense of getting through life but thriving in the midst of every challenge. From the moment I was born, she endured all that motherhood brings. The sleepless nights, the tears, the uncertainty. She sacrificed in ways I didn't even understand until

I became a mother myself. She endured it all with grace, never wavering in her love for me and my brother.

That day was not just a tribute to my mom's life—it was a celebration of everything she had given me. It was a reflection on the life she had lived, the strength she had shown, and the love she had poured out.

I remember how alive she was that night.

Despite the pain, she had been enduring; there was an energy, a joy in her that filled the room. We had fireworks, margaritas, and laughter, and even though it would be our last celebration with her, it felt like the perfect tribute to her life.

The grief of losing my mother came with a deep sense of loss and a question that lingered in my heart: How could I live without her? How could I continue without the woman who had been my guide, my mentor, and my best friend?

It was a question I couldn't answer at first.

But what I did find in the following days was a renewed sense of purpose. I realized that even though my mom was no longer physically here, her legacy lived on through me. The lessons she taught me about love, faith, and endurance became the foundation I leaned on. She had given me everything I needed to keep going, to keep living, to keep honoring her by living with the same strength and love she had shown me.

And in the quiet moments, I began to find peace. It wasn't immediate. It didn't happen overnight. But over time, I realized her death didn't define me. It wasn't the end of our relationship; it was a new chapter. And as I navigated this new phase of life without her, I found a strength within myself I didn't know existed.

In the midst of losing Lindsey and then my mom, I went through a rough patch with my faith. I was angry with God. I didn't understand why I had to lose two people who meant so much to me in such a short period of time. I was bitter, jealous of people who still had their parents, and frustrated by the seeming unfairness of it all.

I felt disconnected from God.

I didn't want to pray.

I didn't want to hear comforting words.

I just wanted the pain to stop.

But then, one day in December, three months after losing Momma, I had a moment of breaking. I realized I carried anger and bitterness God never intended for me to carry. I was holding on to these emotions, letting them fester inside me, and I couldn't do it anymore. I wanted to heal. I wanted to feel whole again. That's when I turned to Psalm 51, a passage I had turned to in the past, and that day, it spoke to me in a way I had never experienced before.

It was in that moment, reading through the Psalm, I began to reconnect with God—not out of obligation but out of a deep desire to heal and to move forward.

That Psalm became my path back to the peace I had once felt. It reignited my relationship with God, but this time, it was different. This time, it was more intimate, more personal, and more profound than it had ever been before. It felt like the weight of my grief was lifted—just a little—and I began to feel like I could breathe again.

I still miss my mom every single day. There are moments when the grief feels fresh, when the pain of losing her hits me in waves. But I've learned grief isn't something we simply get over. It's something we learn to carry. We learn to move forward, to find meaning in the pain, and to keep living with purpose.

Grief doesn't follow a timeline. It doesn't have a set schedule. It doesn't care about your plans. It hits you when you least expect it, and it can take over your world in an instant. But even in those moments of deep sorrow, we have a choice. We can choose to get up, to rise, and to move forward. We can choose to honor the memory of those we've lost by living our lives to the fullest, by carrying the lessons they taught us, and by being present for the people who are still here.

I know my mom's legacy lives on in me. She shaped who I am in ways I didn't fully understand until she was gone. The way she lived, the way she loved, the way she found beauty in the small things—these are the things I carry with me, and these are the things I will continue to pass down to my children, to my friends, and to anyone who needs to hear her story.

As I move forward in life, I remember my mom, and I carry her with me every day. I don't have all the answers. I don't know why life works the way it does. But what I do know is grief doesn't have to defeat us. It doesn't have to break us. It can refine us. It can shape us into better versions of ourselves. And when we choose to rise after loss, we honor the lives of those we've lost, and we create a legacy that will live on far beyond our time.

Grief doesn't have to break us. It's OK to feel lost. It's OK to feel overwhelmed by the pain. But in those moments, we must choose to rise. We must choose to keep moving forward, not because the pain is gone but because we are still here, and we are still capable of making an impact.

Greif changes you. It strips away the illusions, the noise,

and the things that once felt so important. It lays everything bare. And in that raw sacred space you begin to see your life for what it really is . . . a story being written. Losing those who I have loved deeply forced me to confront the parts of my own story I had tucked away. But it also gave me a choice. I could keep carrying the weight in silence, or I could start using my story to bring light to someone else's darkness. That's the thing about grief—it has a way of breaking you, but if you let it, it can also break you free.

CHAPTER 12

Own Your Story

Permission Granted

After everything I've walked through, here's the bottom line of what I've learned: my story matters and your story matters. Every messy, miraculous part of it—*all of it*—has a purpose.

It's easy to believe our experiences are just a series of disconnected moments or our past is something we need to hide. How many times have you thought, *If only I could go back and change that part of my life?*

But here's the truth: every twist, every turn, every detour that felt like a mistake has shaped you into who you are today. And when you embrace those experiences—when you own them instead of running from them—that's where you find your power.

Our stories aren't just for us; they're the roadmap to someone else's breakthrough.

I know it can feel vulnerable to share your journey, especially the raw, unpolished moments you'd rather keep hidden. I used to think my story needed to be perfectly packaged, that I had to present an image of having it all together. I wanted people to see the success, not the struggle. The strength, not the scars. But I didn't truly grow—I didn't truly connect—until

I was willing to be *honest* about my struggles, my fears, and my failures.

It wasn't until I embraced the unfiltered parts of my life that I saw the beauty in them. The moments I once wanted to forget became the very ones deepening my connection with others. And when I started sharing my truth—the real truth, not the polished version—I realized something life-changing: my story isn't just about me.

It is about *who it can help.*

When we stop pretending to be perfect, we give others permission to embrace their own imperfections; that's when something happens.

Owning your story means you stop hiding from it. You stop carrying shame for the things you've walked through. You stop wishing away the parts of your life that shaped you. Every experience—the good, the hard, the painful, and the unexpected—has something to teach us. That failure you feel like you'll never recover from?

It's a stepping stone.

That mistake you made?

It's a lesson wrapped in grace.

That heartbreak, that disappointment, that setback?

It's *not* the end of your story. It's the setup for something greater.

Because nothing in life is wasted.

For me, some of my biggest lessons have come from *pivoting*—from stepping into the unknown when I had no idea what waited for me on the other side. Moving into real estate. Opening my own firm. Leaving behind what was familiar for something that stretched me. Every time I pivoted, I discovered a new part of myself I didn't even know existed. But that kind of discovery doesn't happen when we stay in our comfort zones. It happens when we're willing to take the leap—even when we're scared.

The truth is *growth never happens inside the lines of comfort.*

When I shifted into real estate, it felt like stepping off a ledge. I questioned everything. *What if I fail? What if I'm not good enough?* But here's what I've learned: those fears are just distractions trying to keep us from stepping into something bigger. Every fear, every moment of uncertainty, every doubt was just noise. And when I finally *tuned out the noise* and took the step anyway, I realized something—I was capable of far more than I thought.

And *so are you.*

So if you're in a season of uncertainty, if you feel like you're standing at the edge of a decision, unsure of what's next, I want you to know that it's OK. It's OK to not have all the answers. It's OK to feel afraid.

But what's *not* OK is staying stuck because you're afraid of change.

Staying stuck won't protect you—it will just keep you from growing. You are *not* meant to stay the same. You are *not* meant to live small. Life is a journey of evolution, of uncovering new pieces of yourself, of stepping into the unknown with faith that there is *more.*

I know change can feel overwhelming. But I also know this: the greatest moments of my life didn't come from playing it safe. They came from saying *yes* to the unknown. From believing that what was ahead of me was greater than what was behind me.

So if you're standing at the edge of something new, *take the step.* You don't have to have it all figured out. You just have to *start.*

One of the most powerful stories in the Bible is the story of the woman at the well. She was an outcast, burdened by her past, carrying the weight of shame. She avoided people, drawing water in the heat of the day just so she wouldn't have to face the whispers and judgment of those around her.

She was *hiding*.

And then, in the middle of her mess, Jesus met her right where she was.

He didn't wait for her to clean herself up.

He didn't tell her to fix her life first.

He met her *exactly as she was*—and He offered her something greater.

Grace. Love. Redemption.

And here's what wrecks me every time—her story didn't just change *her*. It changed *others*. She went back to her village and told them about the man who saw her, who *truly* knew her, and because she was willing to share her experience, an entire community was transformed.

Her mess became her message.

And friend, so can yours.

I know it's hard to be vulnerable. I know it feels safer to keep things to yourself.

But what if your story—the parts you wish you could erase—is *exactly* what someone else needs to hear? What if the moment you stop hiding is the moment someone else finds their breakthrough?

I know it's not easy to share your journey, especially the raw, unpolished moments you'd rather keep hidden. If anyone had a reason to bury their past, it was me. I was a teenage mother, still a child myself. I carried the weight of judgment from people who didn't know my heart or my story. I walked through the pain of divorce, the loss of love I thought would last forever. I have failed—more times than I can count.

There were moments when I wanted to erase the hard parts, to rewrite my story in a way that felt more acceptable, more presentable.

But here's the thing—*God doesn't waste a single thing.* Every part of my journey has mattered.

The teenage mother in me? She fought harder than she knew she could. She learned how to love sacrificially before she even fully knew who she was.

> Your story has power; your story has purpose.

The woman who walked through divorce? She discovered her strength in the breaking, found resilience in the rebuilding.

The one who failed over and over? She learned failure is not the end—it's the beginning of something new.

And now, standing on the other side, I can say this with every ounce of confidence in my soul: I *love* my story. I *love* my journey. Not because it was easy, not because I would want to relive the hardest moments, but because *God has redeemed every single part of it.*

I have never been more confident in my own skin than I am today.

Not because my life has been perfect but because I have *owned* it.

I have lived it.

I have walked through the storms and come out stronger, wiser, and full of a peace no one can take from me.

And *that* is why I share my story. Because I want you to know that no matter how broken your past feels, no matter how many wrong turns you've made, you *are not beyond redemption*. You are not too far gone. You are not defined by your mistakes.

What if the very thing you're afraid to share is the thing that could set someone else free?

I want you to hear this: your story, *exactly as it is*, is powerful. The pain, the healing, the struggles, the victories—*all of it*—can be used for something greater than you can imagine.

But only if you're willing to share it.

Only if you're willing to let go of the fear, the shame, the need to look like you have it all together.

Because at the end of the day, people won't remember your perfection. They'll remember your *authenticity*. They'll remember how you made them feel. They'll remember that you showed up, not as someone flawless but as someone *real*.

So, my friend, this is your permission slip.

To own your story.

To *believe* your story matters.

To stop hiding, stop holding back, and start *sharing the message hidden inside your mess*.

You are not defined by what you've walked through. You are *refined* by it.

Your story has *power*.

Your story has *purpose*.

And the moment you own it—the moment you step into it without fear—you become the light helping someone else find their way.

So let's stop hiding. Let's stop pretending. Let's own our stories, share our hearts, and create the kind of impact that lasts long after we're gone.

When you finally own your story – when you stop hiding,

stop editing yourself to be more palatable for the world—you unlock something in you: strength, purpose, clarity. You begin to see everything you walked through wasn't just about survival; it was about preparation. Preparation for the call on your life. The story you've been living? It's not just your past; it's your platform. And that tug you feel deep inside your soul? That relentless whisper that says, "There's more?" That's not just your imagination. That's your calling. And friend, it's time to answer it.

Because *your story matters*. More than you know.

CHAPTER 13

Girl, Get up

Your Calling is Calling

You know, life isn't a destination; it's a journey—a messy, beautiful, sometimes bumpy ride. When I look back at my own path, I see the milestones, the defining moments—some breathtakingly beautiful, others downright painful. But every single one of them shaped me into the woman I am today. It hasn't always been easy, but I wouldn't change a thing. Well, *maybe* a few things (because let's be honest, who wouldn't?) but even those missteps and unexpected detours led me exactly to where I needed to be.

Life has a way of throwing challenges at us, and when it does, we have two choices: let them break us or let them build us.

I choose to let them build me.

And here's the thing—just when you think you've reached the end of a chapter, life hands you a fresh, blank page. It's like picking up a favorite book and realizing there's more to the story than you ever saw before. That's how I see my journey now, and that's how I see yours too.

You're *in* your story right now. Maybe you're in a season of struggle, feeling like the weight of the world is on your shoulders. Or maybe you're soaring, finally stepping into the life you've been working so hard for. Wherever you are, know this—*your story is still being written.* There is more ahead for you than you can imagine.

I won't sugarcoat it—there were times when I thought I had life all figured out, only for everything to shift beneath my feet. I've had moments when I felt certain about where I was headed, only to be thrown into the unknown. I've had to pivot—*not just once, but over and over again.*

Some of those pivots were small, just minor course corrections. But others? They were *huge,* life-altering leaps into the unknown. Walking away from what was comfortable. Stepping into rooms where I wasn't sure I belonged. Leaving behind versions of myself that no longer fit the woman I was becoming. And let me tell you, those pivots weren't always easy. They were scary. They stretched me. But every single one of them was worth it.

Because the truth is growth never happens in the comfort zone.

I've learned that when life presents an opportunity for change, we can either dig in our heels and resist it, or we can lean in and trust that what's ahead is even greater than what we're leaving behind. And every time I've chosen faith over fear, every time I've embraced the pivot, life has surprised me in ways I never could have planned.

And friend, the same is true for you.

Here's what I want you to know—there will be moments when you doubt yourself. When you wonder if you're capable. When you feel like quitting because the road ahead feels too long, too uncertain. But hear me: *you were made for this journey.*

You were made to push through. To rise. To keep going, even when it's hard.

Every challenge you've faced has prepared you for what's next. Every setback has strengthened you. Every heartbreak, every disappointment, every moment that felt like an ending was actually a *beginning in disguise.*

So don't stop now.

Don't stop because it feels uncertain. Don't stop because you're afraid of failing.

You have everything you need inside of you to step forward in confidence. Your past doesn't disqualify you. Your mistakes don't define you. Your *story*—with all of its twists and turns—is the very thing making you who you are.

And if there's one thing I know for sure, it's this: you are stronger than you think.

I've spent a lot of time reflecting on what I want this final chapter to say, and if I could leave you with one thing, it would be this: move forward boldly.

Whatever season you're in—whether you're just getting started, rebuilding, or stepping into something brand new—I want you to trust you're exactly where you need to be. Even if it doesn't make sense yet. Even if it's hard. Because one day, you're going to look back and see that every single step mattered.

One day, you're going to see the moments that felt like breaking points were actually the moments that made you. One day, you're going to realize your story—the one you're still writing—is far more beautiful, far more impactful, and far more meaningful than you ever imagined.

I'm here to remind you that your journey isn't about perfection. It's about embracing the messy, beautiful process of becoming.

The mistakes.

The struggles.

The unexpected twists.

They are all part of what makes you who you are meant to be. So don't shy away from them. Don't hide them. Wear them like badges of honor—because they are.

Let's talk about faith for a moment.

Through every challenge, every heartbreak, every loss—what has kept me going is my faith.

It wasn't always easy to trust. It still isn't. But I've learned faith isn't about having everything figured out or knowing the outcome. It's about taking the next step, even when you're scared. It's about trusting that even in the mess, even in the darkness, there's a light. And that light is guiding you. This journey is not easy. And if anyone tells you it is, they're not being real.

There will be hard days.

Days when you want to curl up and hide.

Days when you wonder if you're even on the right path.

But those days are not the end of your story. They are part of it.

I remember when I lost my best friend, Lindsay. I thought my world had shattered into a million pieces. I had never experienced grief like that before—so raw, so deep. But in the pain, I found a lesson: life is precious.

Lindsay taught me to live fully, to laugh deeply, to embrace the small moments—because they really are the big ones. She didn't wait for perfect moments. She showed up for life, no matter what season she was in.

And then, not long after, I lost my momma. The woman who raised me. Who loved me with everything she had. Believed in me more than I believed in myself. Her passing was another blow to my already bruised heart. But through those losses, I learned something else—I am stronger than I ever realized. I didn't know how much strength I had inside me until I had to find it.

And I'm still here.

I'm still standing.

And so are you.

Here's the truth:

We will all face loss. We will all face challenges that shake us. But those challenges are *not* the end. They are step-ping stones. They are part of the process that makes us who we are meant to be.

> Your story is still unfolding and it's okay if it's not perfect.

Your story is not over yet.

So I'm here to tell you:

Keep going.

Keep rising.

You are *so much stronger* than you realize.

Girl, get up!

Your story is still unfolding, and it's OK if it's not perfect. The beauty is in the journey. In the getting up, over and over again. The beauty is in embracing who you are, where you've been, and where you're going.

Your struggles have shaped you.

Your triumphs have empowered you.

Everything you've been through has prepared you for what's ahead.

So keep dreaming.

Keep believing.

Keep moving forward.

And now, as I bring this book to a close, I want to remind you of the power behind its title: *Girl, Get Up.*

It's more than just a phrase. It's a *declaration.*

It's a reminder that no matter how many times you've felt knocked down, no matter how dark or painful the moment may seem, *you have the strength to rise again.*

Take time to read Mark 5:41-42—the moment when Jesus brought a young girl back to life. She was lying there, lifeless. Her family was mourning, believing it was over.

But Jesus, with a voice full of love and authority, simply said, *"Talitha koum,"* meaning "Little girl, I say to you, get up!"

And *she did.* In that moment, everything changed. Her story didn't end in death—it was just the beginning of a new chapter. And friend, just like her, *you have the ability to rise.* No matter how dead your dreams, your hope, or your spirit may feel at times, remember the call: "Get up, girl."

Life will try to defeat you. But with every setback, there is an opportunity for a *comeback.*

So GET UP.

Step forward. Move boldly into what's next.

Because your story? It matters.

The best is still ahead, and I can't wait to hear all about it!

Connect with Kristi

You got this!

Before you close this book, I want to leave you with something sacred.

In 2024, I received my last Mother's Day card from my mom. We didn't know it would be our final one together. But maybe she did. Inside it, in her unmistakable handwriting, she wrote:

> Get up Girl
> Keep trying . . .
> Keep falling
> Keep Bringing hope
> to a dying world
> Get up Girl.
> Go in the name of
> Jesus. you got this
> Mm

She had said these words to me in countless ways over the years. But seeing them written, just months before she passed, felt like a divine passing of the torch.

And now, I'm passing it to you.

My mom may have been writing to me—but I believe, deep down, she was also writing to you.

So if you need to be reminded one more time:

Keep trying.

Keep falling.

Keep bringing hope.

Get up.

In the name of Jesus—

You got this.

ABOUT THE AUTHOR

Kristi Caudell became a mother at sixteen, and that's where her story truly begins. Not in a boardroom or a classroom, but in the quiet, sacred chaos of figuring life out as a young mom with a fierce will to rise. That early chapter gave her grit, vision, and the ability to see beyond the moment she's in, skills she's carried into every business, every relationship, and every reinvention since.

She's the founder of Lux Exclusives, a first-of-its-kind private platform for high-net-worth individuals to manage, time, and trade their most valuable assets. She's also the visionary behind Rabun Realty, a boutique real estate firm based in the North Georgia mountains where she was raised. Her work in real estate is bold, forward-thinking, and rooted in integrity. But ask her what she's proudest of, and it won't be the deals or the headlines. It will always come back to her family, her faith, and the people she gets to do life with. People are what truly matter to Kristi.

Kristi is also part owner in a few joint ventures that reflect her love for preserving what matters most. She owns a piece of the real estate behind Batesville General, a historic country store turned beloved mountain restaurant, beautifully revived by her dear friend Bonnie Edmonds. It's a place where stories are swapped over biscuits, memories are made over coffee, and history is kept alive one meal at a time. She also owns and operates LakeBurton.com, a platform devoted to all things Lake Burton—where generations gather, lake days are sacred, and roots run deep. It's not just a business, it's part of who she is.

Kristi is a mother, a friend, and the kind of woman who shows up with vision, truth, and probably snacks. Definitely snacks! She's walked through deep grief, heartbreak, and starting over. She's also experienced wild favor, quiet healing, and joy in places she never expected. She doesn't pretend to have it all figured out, but she's built a life she's proud of and makes space for others to do the same.

If you made it to the end of this bio, you're her kind of person. Honest. Hungry. Maybe a little tired but still standing. Kristi is not for everyone, but she is for the woman who's done pretending, who's ready to rise for real, and who understands that sometimes the most powerful thing you can do is simply get back up.